MATERIAL SCIENCE
Volume 2 of 2

MATERIAL SCIENCE

OVERVIEW

The *Material Science* handbook consists of five modules that are contained in two volumes. The following is a brief description of the information presented in each module of the handbook.

Volume 1 of 2

 Module 1 - Structure of Metals

 Explains the basic structure of metals and how those structures are effected by various processes. The module contains information on the various imperfections and defects that the metal may sustain and how they affect the metal.

 Module 2 - Properties of Metals

 Contains information on the properties considered when selecting material for a nuclear facility. Each of the properties contains a discussion on how the property is effected and the metal's application.

Volume 2 of 2

    Module 3 - Thermal Shock

        Contains material relating to thermal stress and thermal shock effects on a system. Explains how thermal stress and shock combined with pressure can cause major damage to components.

    Module 4 - Brittle Fracture

        Contains material on ductile and brittle fracture. These two fractures are the most common in nuclear facilities. Explains how ductile and brittle fracture are effected by the minimum pressurization and temperature curves. Explains the reason why heatup and cooldown rate limits are used when heating up or cooling down the reactor system.

    Module 5 - Plant Materials

        Contains information on the commonly used materials and the characteristics desired when selecting material for use.

The information contained in this handbook is by no means all encompassing. An attempt to present the entire subject of material science would be impractical. However, the *Material Science* handbook does present enough information to provide the reader with a fundamental knowledge level sufficient to understand the advanced theoretical concepts presented in other subject areas, and to better understand basic system operation and equipment operations.

MATERIAL SCIENCE

Module 3

Thermal Shock

TABLE OF CONTENTS

LIST OF FIGURES ii

LIST OF TABLES iii

REFERENCES iv

OBJECTIVES v

THERMAL STRESS 1

    Thermal Shock 1
    Summary 5

PRESSURIZED THERMAL SHOCK 6

    Definition 6
    Evaluating Effects of PTS 6
    Locations of Primary Concern 8
    Summary 8

LIST OF FIGURES

Figure 1 Stress on Reactor Vessel Wall 4

Figure 2 Heatup Stress Profile 7

Figure 3 Cooldown Stress Profile 7

LIST OF TABLES

Table 1 Coefficients of Linear Thermal Expansion 2

REFERENCES

- Academic Program for Nuclear Power Plant Personnel, Volume III, Columbia, MD, General Physics Corporation, Library of Congress Card #A 326517, 1982.

- Foster and Wright, Basic Nuclear Engineering, Fourth Edition, Allyn and Bacon, Inc., 1983.

- Glasstone and Sesonske, Nuclear Reactor Engineering, Third Edition, Van Nostrand Reinhold Company, 1981.

- Reactor Plant Materials, General Physics Corporation, Columbia Maryland, 1982.

- Savannah River Site, Material Science Course, CS-CRO-IT-FUND-10, Rev. 0, 1991.

- Tweeddale, J.G., The Mechanical Properties of Metals Assessment and Significance, American Elsevier Publishing Company, 1964.

- Weisman, Elements of Nuclear Reactor Design, Elsevier Scientific Publishing Company, 1983.

TERMINAL OBJECTIVE

1.0 Without references, **DESCRIBE** the importance of minimizing thermal shock (stress).

ENABLING OBJECTIVES

1.1 **IDENTIFY** the two stresses that are the result of thermal shock (stress) to plant materials.

1.2 **STATE** the two causes of thermal shock.

1.3 Given the material's coefficient of Linear Thermal Expansion, **CALCULATE** the thermal shock (stress) on a material using Hooke's Law.

1.4 **DESCRIBE** why thermal shock is a major concern in reactor systems when rapidly heating or cooling a thick-walled vessel.

1.5 **LIST** the three operational limits that are specifically intended to reduce the severity of thermal shock.

1.6 **DEFINE** the term pressurized thermal shock.

1.7 **STATE** how the pressure in a closed system effects the severity of thermal shock.

1.8 **LIST** the four plant transients that have the greatest potential for causing thermal shock.

1.9 **STATE** the three locations in a reactor system that are of primary concern for thermal shock.

THERMAL STRESS

Thermal stresses arise in materials when they are heated or cooled. Thermal stresses effect the operation of facilities, both because of the large components subject to stress and because they are effected by the way in which the plant is operated. This chapter describes the concerns associated with thermal stress.

EO 1.1 IDENTIFY the two stresses that are the result of thermal shock (stress) to plant materials.

EO 1.2 STATE the two causes of thermal stresses.

EO 1.3 Given the material's coefficient of Linear Thermal Expansion, CALCULATE the thermal stress on a material using Hooke's Law.

EO 1.4 DESCRIBE why thermal stress is a major concern in reactor systems when rapidly heating or cooling a thick-walled vessel.

EO 1.5 LIST the three operational limits that are specifically intended to reduce the severity of thermal shock.

Thermal Shock

Thermal shock (stress) can lead to excessive thermal gradients on materials, which lead to excessive stresses. These stresses can be comprised of *tensile stress*, which is stress arising from forces acting in opposite directions tending to pull a material apart, and *compressive stress*, which is stress arising from forces acting in opposite directions tending to push a material together. These stresses, cyclic in nature, can lead to fatigue failure of the materials.

Thermal shock is caused by nonuniform heating or cooling of a uniform material, or uniform heating of nonuniform materials. Suppose a body is heated and constrained so that it cannot expand. When the temperature of the material increases, the increased activity of the molecules causes them to press against the constraining boundaries, thus setting up thermal stresses.

THERMAL STRESS   Thermal Shock

If the material is not constrained, it expands, and one or more of its dimensions increases. The thermal expansion coefficient (α) relates the fractional change in length $\frac{\Delta l}{l}$, called thermal strain, to the change in temperature per degree ΔT.

$$\alpha = \frac{\frac{\Delta l}{l}}{\Delta T} \tag{3-1}$$

$$\frac{\Delta l}{l} = \alpha \Delta T \tag{3-2}$$

where:

l = length (in.)
Δl = change in length (in.)
α = linear thermal expansion coefficient (°F^{-1})
ΔT = change in temperature (°F)

Table 1 lists the coefficients of linear thermal expansion for several commonly-encountered materials.

TABLE 1
Coefficients of Linear Thermal Expansion

Material	Coefficients of Linear Thermal Expansion (°F^{-1})
Carbon Steel	5.8 x 10^{-6}
Stainless Steel	9.6 x 10^{-6}
Aluminum	13.3 x 10^{-6}
Copper	9.3 x 10^{-6}
Lead	16.3 x 10^{-6}

Thermal Shock   **THERMAL STRESS**

In the simple case where two ends of a material are strictly constrained, the thermal stress can be calculated using Hooke's Law by equating values of $\frac{\Delta l}{l}$ from Equations (3-1), (3-2), and (3-3).

$$E = \frac{stress}{strain} = \frac{F/A}{\frac{\Delta l}{l}} \tag{3-3}$$

or

$$\frac{\Delta l}{l} = \frac{F/A}{E} \tag{3-4}$$

$$\alpha \Delta T = \frac{F/A}{E} \tag{3-5}$$

$$F/A = E\alpha\Delta T$$

where:

F/A = thermal stress (psi)

E = modulus of elasticity (psi)

α = linear thermal expansion coefficient (°F^{-1})

ΔT = change in temperature (°F)

Example: Given a carbon steel bar constrained at both ends, what is the thermal stress when heated from 60°F to 540°F?

Solution:

α = 5.8 x 10^{-6}/°F (from Table 1)

E = 3.0 x 10^7 lb/in.^{2} (from Table 1, Module 2)

ΔT = 540°F - 60°F = 480°F

Stress = F/A = $E\alpha\Delta T$ = (3.0 x 10^7 lb/in.^{2}) x (5.8 x 10^{-6}/°F) x 480°F

Thermal stress = 8.4 x 10^4 lb/in.^{2} (which is higher than the yield point)

THERMAL STRESS   Thermal Shock

Thermal stresses are a major concern in reactor systems due to the magnitude of the stresses involved. With rapid heating (or cooling) of a thick-walled vessel such as the reactor pressure vessel, one part of the wall may try to expand (or contract) while the adjacent section, which has not yet been exposed to the temperature change, tries to restrain it. Thus, both sections are under stress. Figure 1 illustrates what takes place.

A vessel is considered to be thick-walled or thin-walled based on comparing the thickness of the vessel wall to the radius of the vessel. If the thickness of the vessel wall is less than about 1 percent of the vessel's radius, it is usually considered a thin-walled vessel. If the thickness of the vessel wall is more than 5 percent to 10 percent of the vessel's radius, it is considered a thick-walled vessel. Whether a vessel with wall thickness between 1 percent and 5 percent of radius is considered thin-walled or thick-walled depends on the exact design, construction, and application of the vessel.

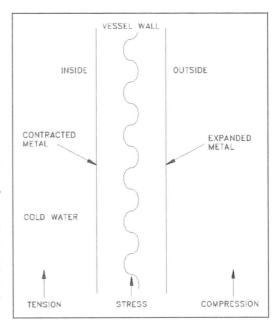

Figure 1 Stress on Reactor Vessel Wall

When cold water enters the vessel, the cold water causes the metal on the inside wall (left side of Figure 1) to cool before the metal on the outside. When the metal on the inside wall cools, it contracts, while the hot metal on the outside wall is still expanded. This sets up a thermal stress, placing the cold side in tensile stress and the hot side in compressive stress, which can cause cracks in the cold side of the wall. These stresses are illustrated in Figure 2 and Figure 3 in the next chapter.

The heatup and cooldown of the reactor vessel and the addition of makeup water to the reactor coolant system can cause significant temperature changes and thereby induce sizable thermal stresses. Slow controlled heating and cooling of the reactor system and controlled makeup water addition rates are necessary to minimize cyclic thermal stress, thus decreasing the potential for fatigue failure of reactor system components.

Operating procedures are designed to reduce both the magnitude and the frequency of these stresses. Operational limitations include heatup and cooldown rate limits for components, temperature limits for placing systems in operation, and specific temperatures for specific pressures for system operations. These limitations permit material structures to change temperature at a more even rate, minimizing thermal stresses.

Summary

The important information in this chapter is summarized below.

Thermal Stress Summary

- Two types of stress that can be caused by thermal shock are:

    Tensile stress
    Compressive stress

- Causes of thermal shock include:

    Nonuniform heating (or cooling) of a uniform material

    Uniform heating (or cooling) of a nonuniform material

- Thermal shock (stress) on a material, can be calculated using Hooke's Law from the following equation. It can lead to the failure of a vessel.

    $$F/A = E\alpha\Delta T$$

- Thermal stress is a major concern due to the magnitude of the stresses involved with rapid heating (or cooling).

- Operational limits to reduce the severity of thermal shock include:

    Heatup and cooldown rate limits

    Temperature limits for placing systems into operation

    Specific temperatures for specific pressures for system operation

---

PRESSURIZED THERMAL SHOCK

Personnel need to be aware how pressure combined with thermal stress can cause failure of plant materials. This chapter addresses thermal shock (stress) with pressure excursions.

> EO 1.6 DEFINE the term pressurized thermal shock.
>
> EO 1.7 STATE how the pressure in a closed system effects the severity of thermal shock.
>
> EO 1.8 LIST the four plant transients that have the greatest potential for causing thermal shock.
>
> EO 1.9 STATE the three locations in a reactor system that are of primary concern for thermal shock.

Definition

One safety issue that is a long-term problem brought on by the aging of nuclear facilities is *pressurized thermal shock* (PTS). PTS is the shock experienced by a thick-walled vessel due to the combined stresses from a rapid temperature and/or pressure change. Nonuniform temperature distribution and subsequent differential expansion and contraction are the causes of the stresses involved. As the facilities get older in terms of full power operating years, the neutron radiation causes a change in the ductility of the vessel material, making it more susceptible to embrittlement. Thus, if an older reactor vessel is cooled rapidly at high pressure, the potential for failure by cracking increases greatly.

Evaluating Effects of PTS

Changes from one steady-state temperature or pressure to another are of interest for evaluating the effects of PTS on the reactor vessel integrity. This is especially true with the changes involved in a rapid cooldown of the reactor system, which causes thermal shock to the reactor vessel. These changes are called transients. Pressure in the reactor system raises the severity of the thermal shock due to the addition of stress from pressure. Transients, which combine high system pressure and a severe thermal shock, are potentially more dangerous due to the added effect of the tensile stresses on the inside of the reactor vessel wall. In addition, the material toughness of the reactor vessel is reduced as the temperature rapidly decreases.

Stresses arising from coolant system pressure exerted against the inside vessel wall (where neutron fluence is greatest) are always tensile in nature. Stresses arising from temperature gradients across the vessel wall can either be tensile or compressive. The type of stress is a function of the wall thickness and reverses from heatup to cooldown. During system heatup, the vessel outer wall temperature lags the inner wall temperature. The stresses produced by this temperature gradient and by system pressure will produce the profile shown in Figure 2.

During heatup, it can be seen that while the pressure stresses are always tensile, at the 1/4 thickness (1/4 T), the temperature stresses are compressive. Thus, the stresses at the 1/4 T location tend to cancel during system heatup. At the 3/4 T location, however, the stresses from both temperature and pressure are tensile and thus, reinforce each other during system heatup. For this reason the 3/4 T location is limiting during system heatup.

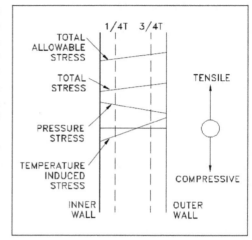

Figure 2 Heatup Stress Profile

During system cooldown, the stress profile of Figure 3 is obtained. During cooldown, the outer wall lags the temperature drop of the inner wall and is at a higher temperature. It can be seen that during cooldown, the stresses at the 3/4 T location are tensile due to system pressure and compressive due to the temperature gradient. Thus during cooldown, the stresses at the 3/4 T location tend to cancel. At the 1/4 T location, however, the pressure and temperature stresses are both tensile and reinforce each other. Thus, the 1/4 T location is limiting during system cooldown.

Plant temperature transients that have the greatest potential for causing thermal shock include excessive plant heatup and cooldown, plant scrams, plant pressure excursions outside of normal pressure bands, and loss of coolant accidents (LOCAs). In pressurized water reactors (PWRs), the two transients that can cause the most severe thermal shock to the reactor pressure vessel are the LOCA with subsequent injection of emergency core cooling system (ECCS) water and a severe increase in the primary-to-secondary heat transfer.

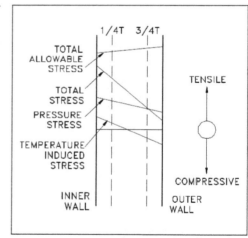

Figure 3 Cooldown Stress Profile

Locations of Primary Concern

Locations in the reactor system, in addition to the reactor pressure vessel, that are primary concerns for thermal shock include the pressurizer spray line and the purification system.

Summary

The important information in this chapter is summarized below.

Pressurized Thermal Shock Summary

- Definition of pressurized thermal shock (PTS)

    Shock experienced by a thick-walled vessel due to the combined stresses from a rapid temperature and/or pressure change.

- Pressure in closed system raises the severity of thermal shock due to the additive effect of thermal and pressure tensile stresses on the inside reactor vessel wall.

- Plant transients with greatest potential to cause PTS include:

    Excessive heatup and cooldown

    Plant scrams

    Plant pressure excursions outside of normal pressure bands

    Loss of coolant accident

- Locations of primary concern for thermal shock are:

    Reactor Vessel

    Pressurizer spray line

    Purification system

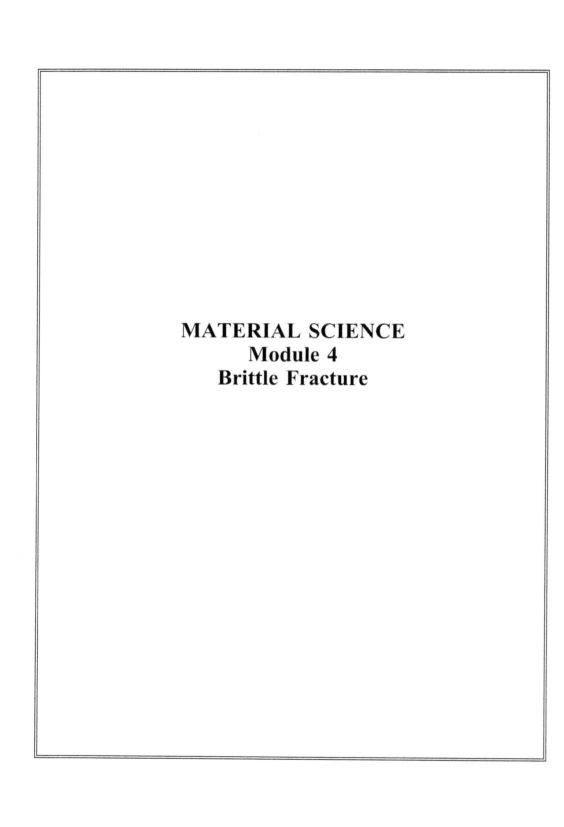

MATERIAL SCIENCE
Module 4
Brittle Fracture

TABLE OF CONTENTS

LIST OF FIGURES	ii
LIST OF TABLES	iii
REFERENCES	iv
OBJECTIVES	v
BRITTLE FRACTURE MECHANISM	1
Brittle Fracture Mechanism	1
Stress-Temperature Curves	3
Crack Initiation and Propagation	4
Fracture Toughness	4
Summary	6
MINIMUM PRESSURIZATION-TEMPERATURE CURVES	7
MPT Definition and Basis	7
Summary	10
HEATUP AND COOLDOWN RATE LIMITS	11
Basis	11
Exceeding Heatup and Cooldown Rates	12
Soak Times	12
Summary	13

LIST OF FIGURES

Figure 1 Basic Fracture Types 2

Figure 2 Stress-Temperature Diagram for Crack Initiation and Arrest 3

Figure 3 Fracture Diagram 5

Figure 4 PCS Temperature vs. Pressure for Normal Operation 8

Figure 5 PCS Temperature vs. Hydrotest Pressure 9

Figure 6 Heatup and Cooldown Rate Limits 11

LIST OF TABLES

NONE

REFERENCES

- *Academic Program for Nuclear Power Plant Personnel*, Volume III, Columbia, MD, General Physics Corporation, Library of Congress Card #A 326517, 1982.

- Foster and Wright, *Basic Nuclear Engineering*, Fourth Edition, Allyn and Bacon, Inc, 1983.

- Glasstone and Sesonske, *Nuclear Reactor Engineering*, Third Edition, Van Nostrand Reinhold Company, 1981.

- *Reactor Plant Materials*, General Physics Corporation, Columbia Maryland, 1982.

- Savannah River Site, *Material Science Course*, CS-CRO-IT-FUND-10, Rev. 0, 1991.

- Tweeddale, J.G., *The Mechanical Properties of Metals Assessment and Significance*, American Elsevier Publishing Company, 1964.

- Weisman, *Elements of Nuclear Reactor Design*, Elsevier Scientific Publishing Company, 1983.

Brittle Fracture | OBJECTIVES

TERMINAL OBJECTIVE

1.0 Without references, **EXPLAIN** the importance of controlling heatup and cooldown rates of the primary coolant system.

ENABLING OBJECTIVES

1.1 **DEFINE** the following terms:

    a. Ductile fracture
    b. Brittle fracture
    c. Nil-ductility Transition (NDT) Temperature

1.2 **DESCRIBE** the two changes made to reactor pressure vessels to decrease NDT.

1.3 **STATE** the effect grain size and irradiation have on a material's NDT.

1.4 **LIST** the three conditions necessary for brittle fracture to occur.

1.5 **STATE** the three conditions that tend to mitigate crack initiation.

1.6 **LIST** the five factors that determine the fracture toughness of a material.

1.7 Given a stress-temperature diagram, **IDENTIFY** the following points:

    a. NDT (with no flaw)
    b. NDT (with flaw)
    c. Fracture transition elastic point
    d. Fracture transition plastic point

1.8 **STATE** the two bases used for developing a minimum pressurization-temperature curve.

1.9 **EXPLAIN** a typical minimum pressure-temperature curve including:

    a. Location of safe operating region
    b. The way the curve will shift due to irradiation

ENABLING OBJECTIVES (Cont.)

1.10 **LIST** the normal actions taken, in sequence, if the minimum pressurization-temperature curve is exceeded during critical operations.

1.11 **STATE** the precaution for hydrostatic testing.

1.12 **IDENTIFY** the basis used for determining heatup and cooldown rate limits.

1.13 **IDENTIFY** the three components that will set limits on the heatup and cooldown rates.

1.14 **STATE** the action typically taken upon discovering the heatup or cooldown rate has been exceeded.

1.15 **STATE** the reason for using soak times.

1.16 **STATE** when soak times become very significant.

Brittle Fracture   *BRITTLE FRACTURE MECHANISM*

BRITTLE FRACTURE MECHANISM

Personnel need to understand brittle fracture. This type of fracture occurs under specific conditions without warning and can cause major damage to plant materials.

EO 1.1   **DEFINE** the following terms:

       a.   **Ductile fracture**   c.   **Nil-ductility Transition**
       b.   **Brittle fracture**   **(NDT) Temperature**

EO 1.2   **DESCRIBE** the two changes made to reactor pressure vessels to decrease NDT.

EO 1.3   **STATE** the effect grain size and irradiation have on a material's NDT.

EO 1.4   **LIST** the three conditions necessary for brittle fracture to occur.

EO 1.5   **STATE** the three conditions that tend to mitigate crack initiation.

EO 1.6   **LIST** the five factors that determine the fracture toughness of a material.

EO 1.7   Given a stress-temperature diagram, **IDENTIFY** the following points:

       a.   **NDT (with no flaw)**   c.   **Fracture transition elastic point**
       b.   **NDT (with flaw)**   d.   **Fracture transition plastic point**

Brittle Fracture Mechanism

Metals can fail by ductile or brittle fracture. Metals that can sustain substantial plastic strain or deformation before fracturing exhibit *ductile fracture*. Usually a large part of the plastic flow is concentrated near the fracture faces.

Metals that fracture with a relatively small or negligible amount of plastic strain exhibit *brittle fracture*. Cracks propagate rapidly. Brittle failure results from *cleavage* (splitting along definite planes). Ductile fracture is better than brittle fracture, because ductile fracture occurs over a period of time, where as brittle fracture is fast, and can occur (with flaws) at lower stress levels than a ductile fracture. Figure 1 shows the basic types of fracture.

BRITTLE FRACTURE MECHANISM

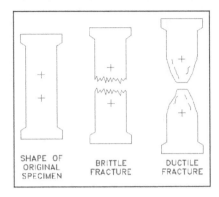

Figure 1 Basic Fracture Types

Brittle cleavage fracture is of the most concern in this module. *Brittle cleavage fracture* occurs in materials with a high strain-hardening rate and relatively low cleavage strength or great sensitivity to multi-axial stress.

Many metals that are ductile under some conditions become brittle if the conditions are altered. The effect of temperature on the nature of the fracture is of considerable importance. Many steels exhibit ductile fracture at elevated temperatures and brittle fracture at low temperatures. The temperature above which a material is ductile and below which it is brittle is known as the *Nil-Ductility Transition (NDT) temperature*. This temperature is not precise, but varies according to prior mechanical and heat treatment and the nature and amounts of impurity elements. It is determined by some form of drop-weight test (for example, the Izod or Charpy tests).

Ductility is an essential requirement for steels used in the construction of reactor vessels; therefore, the NDT temperature is of significance in the operation of these vessels. Small grain size tends to increase ductility and results in a decrease in NDT temperature. Grain size is controlled by heat treatment in the specifications and manufacturing of reactor vessels. The NDT temperature can also be lowered by small additions of selected alloying elements such as nickel and manganese to low-carbon steels.

Of particular importance is the shifting of the NDT temperature to the right (Figure 2), when the reactor vessel is exposed to fast neutrons. The reactor vessel is continuously exposed to fast neutrons that escape from the core. Consequently, during operation the reactor vessel is subjected to an increasing fluence (flux) of fast neutrons, and as a result the NDT temperature increases steadily. It is not likely that the NDT temperature will approach the normal operating temperature of the steel. However, there is a possibility that when the reactor is being shut down or during an abnormal cooldown, the temperature may fall below the NDT value while the internal pressure is still high. The reactor vessel is susceptible to brittle fracture at this point. Therefore, special attention must be given to the effect of neutron irradiation on the NDT temperature of the steels used in fabricating reactor pressure vessels. The Nuclear Regulatory Commission requires that a reactor vessel material surveillance program be conducted in water-cooled power reactors in accordance with ASTM Standards (designation E 185-73).

Pressure vessels are also subject to cyclic stress. *Cyclic stress* arises from pressure and/or temperature cycles on the metal. Cyclic stress can lead to fatigue failure. Fatigue failure, discussed in more detail in Module 5, can be initiated by microscopic cracks and notches and even by grinding and machining marks on the surface. The same (or similar) defects also favor brittle fracture.

Brittle Fracture   BRITTLE FRACTURE MECHANISM

Stress-Temperature Curves

One of the biggest concerns with brittle fracture is that it can occur at stresses well below the yield strength (stress corresponding to the transition from elastic to plastic behavior) of the material, provided certain conditions are present. These conditions are: a flaw such as a crack; a stress of sufficient intensity to develop a small deformation at the crack tip; and a temperature low enough to promote brittle fracture. The relationship between these conditions is best described using a generalized stress-temperature diagram for crack initiation and arrest as shown in Figure 2.

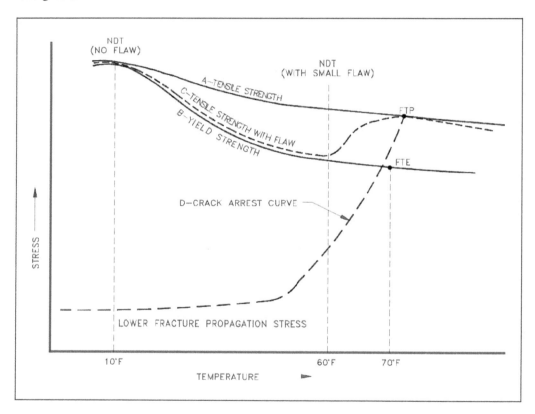

Figure 2 Stress-Temperature Diagram for Crack Initiation and Arrest

Figure 2 illustrates that as the temperature goes down, the tensile strength (Curve A) and the yield strength (Curve B) increase. The increase in tensile strength, sometimes known as the ultimate strength (a maximum of increasing strain on the stress-strain curve), is less than the increase in the yield point. At some low temperature, on the order of 10°F for carbon steel, the yield strength and tensile strength coincide. At this temperature and below, there is no yielding when a failure occurs. Hence, the failure is brittle. The temperature at which the yield and tensile strength coincide is the NDT temperature.

BRITTLE FRACTURE MECHANISM *Brittle Fracture*

When a small flaw is present, the tensile strength follows the dashed Curve C. At elevated temperatures, Curves A and C are identical. At lower temperatures, approximately 50°F above the NDT temperature for material with no flaws, the tensile strength curve drops to the yield curve and then follows the yield curve to lower temperatures. At the point where Curves C and B meet, there is a new NDT temperature. Therefore, if a flaw exists, any failure at a temperature equal or below the NDT temperature for flawed material will be brittle.

Crack Initiation and Propagation

As discussed earlier in this chapter, brittle failure generally occurs because a flaw or crack propagates throughout the material. The start of a fracture at low stresses is determined by the cracking tendencies at the tip of the crack. If a plastic flaw exists at the tip, the structure is not endangered because the metal mass surrounding the crack will support the stress. When brittle fracture occurs (under the conditions for brittle fracture stated above), the crack will initiate and propagate through the material at great speeds (speed of sound). It should be noted that smaller grain size, higher temperature, and lower stress tend to mitigate crack initiation. Larger grain size, lower temperatures, and higher stress tend to favor crack propagation. There is a stress level below which a crack will not propagate at any temperature. This is called the lower fracture propagation stress. As the temperature increases, a higher stress is required for a crack to propagate. The relationship between the temperature and the stress required for a crack to propagate is called the crack arrest curve, which is shown on Figure 2 as Curve D. At temperatures above that indicated on this curve, crack propagation will not occur.

Fracture Toughness

Fracture toughness is an indication of the amount of stress required to propagate a preexisting flaw. The fracture toughness of a metal depends on the following factors.

   a. Metal composition
   b. Metal temperature
   c. Extent of deformations to the crystal structure
   d. Metal grain size
   e. Metal crystalline form

The intersection of the crack arrest curve with the yield curve (Curve B) is called the *fracture transition elastic* (FTE) *point*. The temperature corresponding to this point is normally about 60°F above the NDT temperature. This temperature is also known as the Reference Temperature - Nil-ductility Transition (RT_{NDT}) and is determined in accordance with ASME Section III (1974 edition), NB 2300. The FTE is the temperature above which plastic deformation accompanies all fractures or the highest temperature at which fracture propagation can occur under purely elastic loads. The intersection of the crack arrest curve (Curve D) and the tensile strength or ultimate strength, curve (Curve A) is called the *fracture transition plastic* (FTP) *point*. The temperature corresponding with this point is normally about 120°F above the NDT temperature. Above this temperature, only ductile fractures occur.

Figure 3 is a graph of stress versus temperature, showing fracture initiation curves for various flaw sizes.

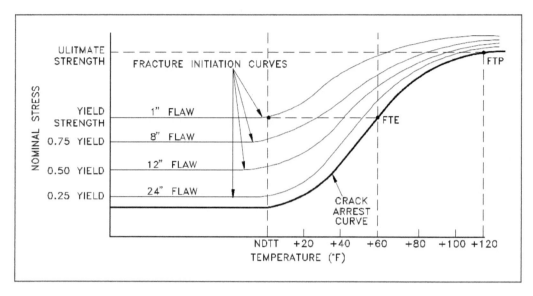

Figure 3 Fracture Diagram

It is clear from the above discussion that we must operate above the NDT temperature to be certain that no brittle fracture can occur. For greater safety, it is desirable that operation be limited above the FTE temperature, or NDT + 60°F. Under such conditions, no brittle fracture can occur for purely elastic loads.

As previously discussed, irradiation of the pressure vessel can raise the NDT temperature over the lifetime of the reactor pressure vessel, restricting the operating temperatures and stress on the vessel. It should be clear that this increase in NDT can lead to significant operating restrictions, especially after 25 years to 30 years of operation where the NDT can raise 200°F to 300°F. Thus, if the FTE was 60°F at the beginning of vessel life and a change in the NDT of 300°F occurred over a period of time, the reactor coolant would have to be raised to more than 360°F before full system pressure could be applied.

Summary

The important information in this chapter is summarized below.

Brittle Fracture Summary

- Ductile fracture is exhibited when metals can sustain substantial plastic strain or deformation before fracturing.

- Brittle fracture is exhibited when metals fracture with a relatively small or negligible amount of plastic strain.

- Nil-Ductility Transition (NDT) temperature is the temperature above which a material is ductile and below which it is brittle.

- Changes made to decrease NDT include:

    Use of smaller grain size in metals

    Small additions of selected alloying elements such as nickel and manganese to low-carbon steels

- NDT decreases due to smaller grain size and increases due to irradiation

- Brittle fracture requires three conditions:

    Flaw such as a crack
    Stress sufficient to develop a small deformation at the crack tip
    Temperature at or below NDT

- Conditions to mitigate crack initiation:

    Smaller grain size
    Higher temperature
    Lower stress levels

- Factors determining fracture toughness of a metal include:

    Metal composition
    Metal temperature
    Extent of deformations to the crystal structure
    Metal grain size
    Metal crystalline form

MINIMUM PRESSURIZATION-TEMPERATURE CURVES

Plant operations are effected by the minimum pressurization-temperature curves. Personnel need to understand the information that is associated with the curves to better operate the plant.

EO 1.8　　STATE the two bases used for developing a minimum pressurization-temperature curve.

EO 1.9　　EXPLAIN a typical minimum pressure-temperature curve including:

　　　　　a.　Location of safe operating region
　　　　　b.　The way the curve will shift due to irradiation

EO 1.10　　LIST the normal actions taken, in sequence, if the minimum pressurization-temperature curve is exceeded during critical operations.

EO 1.11　　STATE the precaution for hydrostatic testing.

MPT Definition and Basis

Minimum pressurization-temperature (MPT) *curves* specify the temperature and pressure limitations for reactor plant operation. They are based on reactor vessel and head stress limitations and the need to preclude reactor vessel and head brittle fracture. Figure 4 shows some pressure-temperature operating curves for a pressurized water reactor (PWR) Primary Coolant System (PCS).

Note that the safe operating region is to the right of the reactor vessel MPT curve. The reactor vessel MPT curve ensures adequate operating margin away from the crack arrest curve discussed above. The curves used by operations also incorporate instrument error to ensure adequate safety margin. Because of the embrittling effects of neutron irradiation, the MPT curve will shift to the right over core life to account for the increased brittleness or decreased ductility. Figure 4 also contains pressurizer and steam generator operating curves. Operating curves may also include surge line and primary coolant pump operating limitations. The MPT relief valve setting prevents exceeding the NDT limit for pressure when the PCS is cold and is set below the lowest limit of the reactor vessel MPT curve.

MINIMUM PRESSURIZATION-TEMPERATURE CURVES

Brittle Fracture

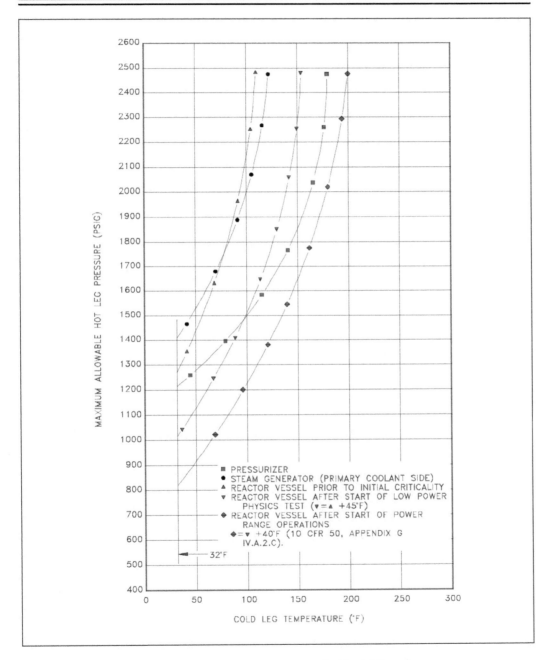

Figure 4 PCS Temperature vs. Pressure for Normal Operation

If the limit of the MPT curve is exceeded during critical operation, the usual action is to scram the reactor, cool down and depressurize the PCS, and conduct an engineering evaluation prior to further plant operation.

During hydrostatic testing, minimum pressurization temperature precautions include making sure that desired hydrostatic pressure is consistent with plant temperatures so that excessive stress does not occur. Figure 5 shows MPT curves for hydrostatic testing of a PWR PCS. The safe operating region is to the right of the MPT curves. Other special hydrostatic limits may also apply during testing.

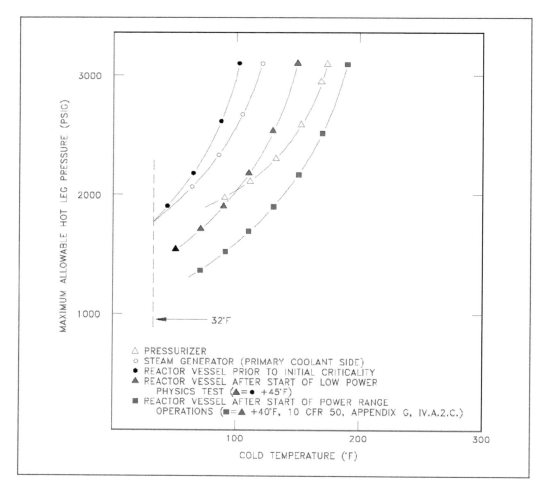

Figure 5 PCS Temperature vs. Hydrotest Pressure

MINIMUM
PRESSURIZATION-TEMPERATURE CURVES   *Brittle Fracture*

Summary

The important information in this chapter is summarized below.

Minimum Pressurization-Temperature Curves Summary

- MPT curves are based on reactor vessel and head stress limitations, and the need to prevent reactor vessel and head brittle fracture.

- MPT curve safe operating region is to the right of the curve.

- MPT curve will shift to the right due to irradiation.

- Normal actions if MPT curves are exceeded during critical operation are:

    Scram reactor

    Cool down and depressurize

    Conduct engineering evaluation prior to further plant operation

- The precaution to be observed when performing a hydrostatic test is to make sure the pressure is consistent with plant temperatures.

HEATUP AND COOLDOWN RATE LIMITS

Personnel operating a reactor plant must be aware of the heatup and cooldown rates for the system. If personnel exceed these rates, major damage could occur under certain conditions.

EO 1.12   IDENTIFY the basis used for determining heatup and cooldown rate limits.

EO 1.13   IDENTIFY the three components that will set limits on the heatup and cooldown rates.

EO 1.14   STATE the action typically taken upon discovering the heatup or cooldown rate has been exceeded.

EO 1.15   STATE the reason for using soak times.

EO 1.16   STATE when soak times become very significant.

Basis

Heatup and cooldown rate limits, as shown in Figure 6, are based upon the impact on the future fatigue life of the plant. The heatup and cooldown limits ensure that the plant's fatigue life is equal to or greater than the plant's operational life. Large components such as flanges, the reactor vessel head, and even the reactor vessel itself are the limiting components. Usually the most limiting component will set the heatup and cooldown rates.

Thermal stress imposed by a rapid temperature change (a fast ramp or even a step change) of approximately 20°F (depending upon the plant) is insignificant (10^6 cycles allowed depending upon component) and has no effect on the design life of the plant.

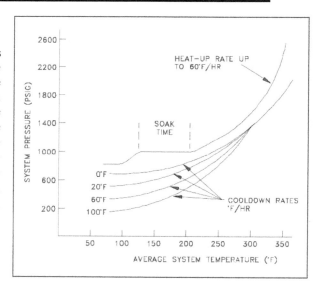

Figure 6 Heatup and Cooldown Rate Limits

Exceeding Heatup and Cooldown Rates

Usually, exceeding heatup or cooldown limits or other potential operational thermal transient limitations is not an immediate hazard to continued operation and only requires an assessment of the impact on the future fatigue life of the plant. However, this may depend upon the individual plant and its limiting components.

Individual components, such as the pressurizer, may have specific heatup and cooldown limitations that, in most cases, are less restrictive than for the PCS.

Because of the cooldown transient limitations of the PCS, the reactor should be shut down in an orderly manner. Cooldown of the PCS from full operating temperature to 200°F or less requires approximately 24 hours (depending upon cooldown limit rates) as a minimum. Requirements may vary from plant to plant.

Soak Times

Soak times may be required when heating up the PCS, especially when large limiting components are involved in the heatup. Soak times are used so that heating can be carefully controlled. In this manner thermal stresses are minimized. An example of a soak time is to heat the reactor coolant to a specified temperature and to stay at that temperature for a specific time period. This allows the metal in a large component, such as the reactor pressure vessel head, to heat more evenly from the hot side to the cold side, thus limiting the thermal stress across the head. Soak time becomes very significant when the PCS is at room temperature or below and very close to its RT_{NDT} temperature limitations.

Brittle Fracture   *HEATUP AND COOLDOWN RATE LIMITS*

Summary

The important information in this chapter is summarized below.

Heatup-Cooldown Rate Limits Summary

- Heatup and cooldown rate limits are based upon impact on the future fatigue life of the plant. The heatup and cooldown rate limits ensure that the plant's fatigue life is equal to or greater than the plant's operational life.

- Large components such as flanges, reactor vessel head, and the vessel itself are the limiting components.

- Usually exceeding the heatup or cooldown rate limits requires only an assessment of the impact on the future fatigue life of the plant.

- Soak times:

    May be required when heating large components

    Used to minimize thermal stresses by controlling the heating rate

    Become very significant if system is at room temperature or below and very close to RT_{NDT} temperature limitations

---

Rev. 0   MS-04

Intentionally Left Blank.

MATERIAL SCIENCE
Module 5
Plant Materials

Plant Materials   TABLE OF CONTENTS

TABLE OF CONTENTS

LIST OF FIGURES iv

LIST OF TABLES v

REFERENCES vi

OBJECTIVES vii

PROPERTIES CONSIDERED
WHEN SELECTING MATERIALS 1

    Overview 1
    Material Properties 1
    Summary 4

FUEL MATERIALS 5

    Overview of Material Types 5
    Plutonium 5
    Uranium 6
    Thorium 7
    Nuclear Fuel Selection 8
    Summary 10

CLADDING AND REFLECTORS 11

    Cladding 11
    Reflector Materials 12
    Summary 14

CONTROL MATERIALS 15

    Overview of Poisons 15
    Hafnium 15
    Silver-Indium-Cadmium Alloys 15
    Boron-Containing Materials 16
    Summary 17

TABLE OF CONTENTS (Cont.)

SHIELDING MATERIALS 18

    Overview 18
    Neutron Radiation 18
    Gamma Radiation 19
    Alpha and Beta Radiation 20
    Summary 21

NUCLEAR REACTOR CORE PROBLEMS 22

    Fuel Pellet-Cladding Interaction 22
    Fuel Densification 23
    Fuel Cladding Embrittlement 24
    Effects on Fuel Due to Swelling and Core Burnup 24
    Summary 25

PLANT MATERIAL PROBLEMS 27

    Fatigue Failure 27
    Work (Strain) Hardening 28
    Creep 29
    Summary 31

ATOMIC DISPLACEMENT DUE TO IRRADIATION 32

    Overview 32
    Atomic Displacements 33
    Summary 34

THERMAL AND DISPLACEMENT SPIKES DUE TO IRRADIATION 35

    Thermal Spikes 35
    Displacement Spikes 35
    Summary 36

EFFECT DUE TO NEUTRON CAPTURE 37

    Effect Due to Neutron Capture 37
    Physical Effects of Radiation 39
    Summary 44

TABLE OF CONTENTS (Cont.)

RADIATION EFFECTS IN ORGANIC COMPOUNDS 45

    Radiation Effects 45
    Summary 48

REACTOR USE OF ALUMINUM 49

    Applications 49
    Summary 51

LIST OF FIGURES

Figure 1 Nominal Stress-Strain Curve vs True Stress-Strain Curve 29

Figure 2 Successive Stage of Creep with Increasing Time 30

Figure 3 Thermal and Fast Neutrons Interactions with a Solid 33

Figure 4 Qualitative Representation of Neutron Irradiation Effect on Many Metals 40

Figure 5 Increase in NDT Temperatures of Steels from Irradiation Below 232°C 42

Figure 6 (a) Growth of Uranium Rod; (b) Uranium Rod Size Dummy 43

Figure 7 Effect of Gamma Radiation on Different Types of Hydrocarbon 47

Figure 8 Effect of Irradiation on Tensile Properties of 2SO Aluminum 50

LIST OF TABLES

Table 1 General Effects of Fast-Neutron Irradiation on Metals 39

Table 2 Effect of Fast-Neutron Irradiation on the Mechanical Properties of Metals 41

Table 3 Radiolytic Decomposition of Polyphenyls at 350°C 48

REFERENCES

- Academic Program for Nuclear Power Plant Personnel, Volume III, Columbia, MD, General Physics Corporation, Library of Congress Card #A 326517, 1982.

- Foster and Wright, Basic Nuclear Engineering, Fourth Edition, Allyn and Bacon, Inc., 1983.

- Glasstone and Sesonske, Nuclear Reactor Engineering, Third Edition, Van Nostrand Reinhold Company, 1981.

- Reactor Plant Materials, General Physics Corporation, Columbia Maryland, 1982.

- Savannah River Site, Material Science Course, CS-CRO-IT-FUND-10, Rev. 0, 1991.

- Tweeddale, J.G., The Mechanical Properties of Metals Assessment and Significance, American Elsevier Publishing Company, 1964.

- Weisman, Elements of Nuclear Reactor Design, Elsevier Scientific Publishing Company, 1983.

Plant Materials OBJECTIVES

TERMINAL OBJECTIVE

1.0   Without references, **DESCRIBE** the considerations commonly used when selecting material for use in a reactor plant.

ENABLING OBJECTIVES

1.1   **DEFINE** the following terms:

    a.   Machinability
    b.   Formability
    c.   Stability
    d.   Fabricability

1.2   **IDENTIFY** the importance of a material property and its application in a reactor plant.

1.3   **LIST** the four radioactive materials that fission by thermal neutrons and are used as reactor fuels.

1.4   **STATE** the four considerations in selecting fuel material and the desired effect on the nuclear properties of the selected fuel material.

1.5   **STATE** the four major characteristics necessary in a material used for fuel cladding.

1.6   **IDENTIFY** the four materials suitable for use as fuel cladding material and their applications.

1.7   **STATE** the purpose of a reflector.

1.8   **LIST** the five essential requirements for reflector material in a thermal reactor.

1.9   **STATE** the five common poisons used as control rod material.

1.10 **IDENTIFY** the advantage(s) and/or disadvantages of the five common poisons used as control rod material.

OBJECTIVES	Plant Materials

ENABLING OBJECTIVES (Cont.)

1.11 **DESCRIBE** the requirements of a material used to shield against the following types of radiation:

    a.   Beta
    b.   Gamma
    c.   High energy neutron
    d.   Low energy neutron

1.12 **STATE** the nuclear reactor core problems and causes associated with the following:

    a.   Pellet-cladding interaction
    b.   Fuel densification
    c.   Fuel cladding embrittlement
    d.   Fuel burnup and fission product swelling

1.13 **STATE** the measures taken to counteract or minimize the effects of the following:

    a.   Pellet-cladding interaction
    b.   Fuel densification
    c.   Fuel cladding embrittlement
    d.   Fission product swelling of a fuel element

1.14 **DEFINE** the following terms:

    a.   Fatigue failure
    b.   Work hardening
    c.   Creep

1.15 **STATE** the measures taken to counteract or minimize the effects of the following:

    a.   Fatigue failure
    b.   Work hardening
    c.   Creep

Plant Materials   *OBJECTIVES*

ENABLING OBJECTIVES (Cont.)

1.16 **STATE** how the following types of radiation interact with metals:

     a. Gamma
     b. Alpha
     c. Beta
     d. Fast neutron
     e. Slow neutron

1.17 **DEFINE** the following terms:

     a. Knock-on
     b. Vacancy
     c. Interstitial

1.18 **DEFINE** the following terms:

     a. Thermal spike
     b. Displacement spike

1.19 **STATE** the effect a large number of displacement spikes has on the properties of a metal.

1.20 **DESCRIBE** how the emission of radiation can cause dislocation of the atom emitting the radiation.

1.21 **STATE** the two effects on a crystalline structure resulting from the capture of a neutron.

1.22 **STATE** how thermal neutrons can produce atomic displacements.

1.23 **STATE** how gamma and beta radiation effect organic materials.

1.24 **IDENTIFY** the change in organic compounds due to radiation.

     a. Nylon
     b. High-density polyethylene marlex 50
     c. Rubber

1.25 **IDENTIFY** the chemical bond with the least resistance to radiation.

1.26 **DEFINE** the term polymerization.

ENABLING OBJECTIVES (Cont.)

1.27 **STATE** the applications and the property that makes aluminum desirable in reactors operating at:

   a. Low kilowatt power
   b. Low temperature ranges
   c. Moderate temperature range

1.28 **STATE** why aluminum is undesirable in high temperature power reactors.

Plant Materials   PROPERTIES CONSIDERED WHEN SELECTING MATERIALS

PROPERTIES CONSIDERED WHEN SELECTING MATERIALS

There are many different kinds of materials used in the construction of a nuclear facility. Once constructed, these materials are subjected to environments and operating conditions that may lead to material problems. This chapter discusses considerations for selection and application of plant materials.

EO 1.1   DEFINE the following terms:

        a.   Machinability   c.   Stability
        b.   Formability   d.   Fabricability

EO 1.2   IDENTIFY the importance of a material property and its application in a reactor plant.

Overview

During the selection and application of materials used for construction of a nuclear facility, many different material properties and factors must be considered depending upon the requirements for each specific application. Generally, these consist of both non-fuel reactor materials, used for structural and component construction, and fuel materials. This chapter discusses some of the considerations used in the selection process for plant materials including material properties, fuel, fuel cladding, reflector material, control materials, and shielding materials.

Material Properties

The following properties are considered when selecting materials that are to be used in the construction of nuclear facilities.

Machinability

Components may be formed by removing metal "chips" by mechanical deformation. This process is referred to as machining. *Machinability* describes how a metal reacts to mechanical deformation by removing chips, with respect to the amount of metal effectively removed and the surface finish attainable. The mechanical properties of the metal will be the factors that influence the machinability of a metal.

Many components used in nuclear reactor construction use machined parts that require very close tolerances and very smooth surfaces. Thus, machinability becomes an important consideration when choosing materials for manufacturing these parts.

Rev. 0   Page 1   MS-05

Formability

Components may be formed by processes such as rolling or bending, which may cause some parts of the metal to expand more than others. *Formability* of a material is its ability to withstand peripheral expansion without failure or the capacity of the material to be to manufactured into the final required shape. This becomes important in selecting materials that have to be made into specific shapes by such means as rolling or bending and still retain their required strength.

Ductility

Ductility is the plastic response to tensile force. Plastic response, or plasticity, is particularly important when a material is to be formed by causing the material to flow during the manufacture of a component. It also becomes important in components that are subject to tension and compression, at every temperature between the lowest service temperature and the highest service temperature. Ductility is essential for steels used in construction of reactor pressure vessels. Ductility is required because the vessel is subjected to pressure and temperature stresses that must be carefully controlled to preclude brittle fracture. Brittle fracture is discussed in more detail in Module 4, Brittle Fracture.

Stability

Stability of a material refers to its mechanical and chemical inertness under the conditions to which it will be subjected. Nuclear plants have a variety of environments to which materials are subjected. Some of these environments, such as high temperatures, high acid, high radiation, and high pressure, can be considered extreme and harsh; therefore, the stability of the materials selected for service in these areas is a major consideration.

Corrosion mechanisms can become very damaging if not controlled. They are identified in Module 2, Properties of Metals. High corrosion resistance is desirable in reactor systems because low corrosion resistance leads to increased production of corrosion products that may be transported through the core. These products become irradiated and contaminate the entire system. This contamination contributes to high radiation levels after shutdown. For these reasons, corrosion resistant materials are specially chosen for use in the primary and secondary coolant systems.

Availability

The *availability* of a material used in the construction of nuclear plants refers to the ease with which a material can be obtained and its cost.

Fabricability

Fabricability is a measure of the ease with which a material can be worked and made into desirable shapes and forms. Many components of a nuclear reactor have very complicated shapes and forms and require very close tolerances. Therefore, fabricability is an important consideration in the manufacturing of these components.

Heat Transfer

Good heat transfer properties are desirable from the fuel boundary to the coolant in order that the heat produced will be efficiently transferred.

For a constant amount of heat transfer, a degraded heat transfer characteristic requires higher fuel temperature, which is not desirable. Therefore, desirable heat transfer properties in the selection of reactor materials, especially those used as core cladding and heat exchanger tubes, are a major consideration.

Cost

Capital costs for building a typical nuclear facility can be millions of dollars. A major portion of the cost is for plant material; therefore, cost is an important factor in the selection of plant materials.

Mechanical Strength

Preventing release of radioactive fission products is a major concern in the design, construction, and operation of a nuclear plant. Therefore, mechanical strength plays an important role in selecting reactor materials. High mechanical strength is desirable because of its possible degradation due to radiation damage and the need to contain the radioactive liquids and fuel.

Summary

The important information in this chapter is summarized below.

Material Properties Considered for Selection Summary

- Machinability is the ability of a metal to react to mechanical deformation by removing chips, with respect to the amount of metal effectively removed and the surface finish attainable. This property is important when selecting parts that require very close tolerances and very smooth surfaces.

- Formability of a material is its ability to withstand peripheral expansion without failure or the capacity of the material to be manufactured into the final required shape. This property is important when selecting materials that have to be made into specific shapes by such means as rolling or bending and still retain their required strength.

- Stability of a material refers to its mechanical and chemical inertness under the conditions to which it will be subjected. This property is important when selecting materials environments such as high temperature, high acid, high radiation, and high pressure environments.

- Fabricability is a measure of the ease with which a material can be worked and made into desirable shapes and forms. This property is important when materials are required to have very complicated shapes or forms and require very close tolerances.

- Ductility is essential for materials that are subject to tensile and compressive stresses. Ductility is important in the construction of reactor vessels.

- Availability is the ease with which material can be obtained and its cost.

- Good heat transfer properties are desirable for the boundary between the fuel and the coolant. These properties are desirable for heat exchanger tubes, fuel cladding, etc.

- Cost is an important factor in selecting plant materials.

FUEL MATERIALS

Nuclear plants require radioactive material to operate. Certain metals that are radioactive can be used to produce and sustain the nuclear reaction. This chapter discusses the materials used in the various nuclear applications. The student should refer to the Nuclear Physics and Reactor Theory Fundamentals Handbook prior to continuing to better understand the material in this chapter.

EO 1.3   **LIST the four radioactive materials that fission by thermal neutrons and are used as reactor fuels.**

EO 1.4   **STATE the four considerations in selecting fuel material and the desired effect on the nuclear properties of the selected fuel material.**

Overview of Material Types

The reactor core is the heart of any nuclear reactor and consists of fuel elements made of a suitable fissile material. There are presently four radioactive materials that are suitable for fission by thermal neutrons. They are uranium-233 (^{233}U), uranium-235 (^{235}U), plutonium-239 (^{239}Pu), and plutonium-241 (^{241}Pu). The isotopes uranium-238 (^{238}U) and thorium-232 (^{232}Th) are fissionable by fast neutrons. The following text discusses plutonium, uranium, and thorium as used for nuclear fuel.

Plutonium

Plutonium is an artificial element produced by the transmutation of ^{238}U. It does exist in small amounts (5 parts per trillion) in uranium ore, but this concentration is not high enough to be mined commercially.

Plutonium is produced by the conversion of ^{238}U into ^{239}Pu according to the following reaction.

$$^{238}_{92}U + ^{1}_{0}n \rightarrow ^{239}_{92}U \xrightarrow{\beta^-} ^{239}_{93}Np \xrightarrow{\beta^-} ^{239}_{94}Pu$$

This reaction occurs in reactors designed specifically to produce fissionable fuel. These reactors are frequently called breeder reactors because they produce more fissionable fuel than is used in the reaction. Plutonium is also produced in thermal ^{235}U reactors that contain ^{238}U. Plutonium can be obtained through the processing of spent fuel elements. To be useful as a fuel, plutonium must be alloyed to be in a stable phase as a metal or a ceramic.

Plutonium dioxide (PuO$_2$) is the most common form used as a reactor fuel. PuO$_2$ is not used alone as a reactor fuel; it is mixed with uranium dioxide. This mixture ranges from 20% plutonium dioxide for fast reactor fuel to 3% to 5% for thermal reactors.

Plutonium-239 can serve as the fissile material in both thermal and fast reactors. In thermal reactors, the plutonium-239 produced from uranium-238 can provide a partial replacement for uranium-235. The use of plutonium-239 in fast reactors is much more economical, because breeding takes place, which results in the production of more plutonium-239 than is consumed by fission.

Uranium

The basic nuclear reactor fuel materials used today are the elements uranium and thorium. Uranium has played the major role for reasons of both availability and usability. It can be used in the form of pure metal, as a constituent of an alloy, or as an oxide, carbide, or other suitable compound. Although metallic uranium was used as a fuel in early reactors, its poor mechanical properties and great susceptibility to radiation damage excludes its use for commercial power reactors today. The source material for uranium is uranium ore, which after mining is concentrated in a "mill" and shipped as an impure form of the oxide U$_3$O$_8$ (yellow cake). The material is then shipped to a materials plant where it is converted to uranium dioxide (UO$_2$), a ceramic, which is the most common fuel material used in commercial power reactors. The UO$_2$ is formed into pellets and clad with zircaloy (water-cooled reactors) or stainless steel (fast sodium-cooled reactors) to form fuel elements. The cladding protects the fuel from attack by the coolant, prevents the escape of fission products, and provides geometrical integrity.

Oxide fuels have demonstrated very satisfactory high-temperature, dimensional, and radiation stability and chemical compatibility with cladding metals and coolant in light-water reactor service. Under the much more severe conditions in a fast reactor, however, even inert UO$_2$ begins to respond to its environment in a manner that is often detrimental to fuel performance. Uranium dioxide is almost exclusively used in light-water-moderated reactors (LWR). Mixed oxides of uranium and plutonium are used in liquid-metal fast breeder reactors (LMFBR).

The major disadvantages of oxide fuels that have prompted the investigation of other fuel materials are their low uranium density and low thermal conductivity that decreases with increasing temperatures. The low density of uranium atoms in UO$_2$ requires a larger core for a given amount of fissile species than if a fuel of higher uranium density were used. The increase in reactor size with no increase in power raises the capital cost of the reactor. Poor thermal conductivity means that the centerline temperature of the fuel and the temperature difference between the center and the surface of the fuel rod must be very large for sufficient fission heat be extracted from a unit of fuel to make electric power production economical. On the other hand, central fuel temperatures close to the melting point have a beneficial fission product scouring effect on the fuel.

Thorium

Natural thorium consists of one isotope, ^{232}Th, with only trace quantities of other much more radioactive thorium isotopes. The only ore mineral of thorium, that is found in useful amounts is monazite. Monazite-bearing sands provide most commercial supplies. The extraction and purification of thorium is carried out in much the same manner as for uranium. Thorium dioxide (ThO$_2$) is used as the fuel of some reactors. Thorium dioxide can be prepared by heating thorium metal or a wide variety of other thorium compounds in air. It occurs typically as a fine white powder and is extremely refractory (hard to melt or work) and resistant to chemical attack.

The sole reason for using thorium in nuclear reactors is the fact that thorium (^{232}Th) is not fissile, but can be converted to uranium-233 (fissile) via neutron capture. Uranium-233 is an isotope of uranium that does not occur in nature. When a thermal neutron is absorbed by this isotope, the number of neutrons produced is sufficiently larger than two, which permits breeding in a thermal nuclear reactor. No other fuel can be used for thermal breeding applications. It has the superior nuclear properties of the thorium fuel cycle when applied in thermal reactors that motivated the development of thorium-based fuels. The development of the uranium fuel cycle preceded that of thorium because of the natural occurrence of a fissile isotope in natural uranium, uranium-235, which was capable of sustaining a nuclear chain reaction. Once the utilization of uranium dioxide nuclear fuels had been established, development of the compound thorium dioxide logically followed.

As stated above, thorium dioxide is known to be one of the most refractory and chemically nonreactive solid substances available. This material has many advantages over uranium dioxide. Its melting point is higher; it is among the highest measured. It is not subject to oxidation beyond stoichiometric (elements entering into and resulting from combination) ThO$_2$. At comparable temperatures over most of the expected operating range its thermal conductivity is higher than that of UO$_2$. One disadvantage is that the thorium cycle produces more fission gas per fission, although experience has shown that thorium dioxide is superior to uranium dioxide in retaining these gases. Another disadvantage is the cost of recycling thoria-base fuels, or the "spiking" of initial-load fuels with ^{233}U. It is more difficult because ^{233}U always contains ^{232}U as a contaminant. ^{232}U alpha decays to ^{228}Th with a 1.9 year half-life. The decay chain of ^{228}Th produces strong gamma and alpha emitters. All handling of such material must be done under remote conditions with containment.

Investigation and utilization of thorium dioxide and thorium dioxide-uranium dioxide (thoria-urania) solid solutions as nuclear fuel materials have been conducted at the Shipping port Light Water Breeder Reactor (LWBR). After a history of successful operation, the reactor was shut down on October 1, 1982. Other reactor experience with ThO$_2$ and ThO$_2$-UO$_2$ fuels have been conducted at the Elk River (Minnesota) Reactor, the Indian Point (N.Y.) No. 1 Reactor, and the HTGR (High-temperature Gas-cooled Reactor) at Peach Bottom, Pennsylvania, and at Fort St. Vrain, a commercial HTGR in Colorado.

As noted above, interest in thorium as a contributor to the world's useful energy supply is based on its transmutability into the fissile isotope ^{233}U. The ease with which this property can be utilized depends on the impact of the nuclear characteristics of thorium on the various reactor systems in which it might be placed and also on the ability to fabricate thorium into suitable fuel elements and, after irradiation, to separate chemically the resultant uranium. The nuclear characteristics of thorium are briefly discussed below by comparing them with ^{238}U as a point of reference.

First, a higher fissile material loading requirement exists for initial criticality for a given reactor system and fissile fuel when thorium is used than is the case for an otherwise comparable system using ^{238}U.

Second, on the basis of nuclear performance, the interval between refueling for comparable thermal reactor systems can be longer when thorium is the fertile fuel. However, for a given reactor system, fuel element integrity may be the limiting factor in the depletion levels that can be achieved.

Third, ^{233}Pa (protactinium), which occurs in the transmutation chain for the conversion of thorium to ^{233}U, acts as a power history dependent neutron poison in a thorium-fueled nuclear reactor. There is no isotope with comparable properties present in a ^{238}U fuel system.

Fourth, for comparable reactor systems, the one using a thorium-base fuel will have a larger negative feedback on neutron multiplication with increased fuel temperature (Doppler coefficient) than will a ^{238}U-fueled reactor.

Fifth, for comparable reactor configurations, a ^{232}Th/^{233}U fuel system will have a greater stability relative to xenon-induced power oscillations than will a ^{238}U/^{235}U fuel system. The stability is also enhanced by the larger Doppler coefficient for the ^{232}Th/^{233}U fuel system.

And sixth, the effective value of β for ^{232}Th/^{233}U systems is about half that of ^{235}U-fueled reactors and about the same as for plutonium-fueled reactors. A small value of β means that the reactor is more responsive to reactivity changes.

In conclusion, the nuclear properties of thorium can be a source of vast energy production. As demonstrated by the Light Water Breeder Reactor Program, this production can be achieved in nuclear reactors utilizing proven light water reactor technology.

Nuclear Fuel Selection

The nuclear properties of a material must be the first consideration in the selection of a suitable nuclear fuel. Principle properties are those bearing on neutron economy: absorption and fission cross sections, the reactions and products that result, neutron production, and the energy released. These are properties of a specific nuclide, such as ^{232}Th, and its product during breeding, ^{233}U. To assess these properties in the performance of the bulk fuel, the density value, or frequency of occurrence per unit volume, of the specific nuclide must be used.

Once it has been established that the desired nuclear reaction is feasible in a candidate fuel material, the effect of other material properties on reactor performance must be considered. For the reactor to perform its function of producing usable energy, the energy must be removed. It is desirable for thermal conductivity to be as high as possible throughout the temperature range of operations and working life of the reactor. High thermal conductivity allows high power density and high specific power without excessive fuel temperature gradients. The selection of a ceramic fuel represents a compromise. Though it is known that thermal conductivities comparable to those of metals cannot be expected, chemical and dimensional stability at high temperature are obtained.

Because the thermal conductivity of a ceramic fuel is not high, it is necessary to generate relatively high temperatures at the centers of ceramic fuel elements. A high melting point enables more energy to be extracted, all other things being equal. In all cases, the fuel must remain well below the melting point in normal operation, but a higher melting point results in a higher permissible operating temperature.

The dimensional stability of the fuel under conditions of high temperature and high burnup is of primary importance in determining the usable lifetime. The dimensional stability is compromised by swelling, which constricts the coolant channels and may lead to rupture of the metal cladding and escape of highly radioactive fission products into the coolant. The various other factors leading to the degradation of fuel performance as reactor life proceeds (the exhaustion of fissionable material, the accumulation of nonfissionable products, the accumulation of radiation effects on associated nonfuel materials) are all of secondary importance in comparison to dimensional stability of the fuel elements.

The main cause of fuel element swelling is the accumulation of two fission product atoms for each atom fissioned. This is aggravated by the fact that some of the fission products are gases. The ability of a ceramic fuel to retain and accommodate fission gases is therefore of primary importance in determining core lifetime.

The chemical properties of a fuel are also important considerations. A fuel should be able to resist the wholesale change in its properties, or the destruction of its mechanical integrity, that might take place if it is exposed to superheated coolant water through a cladding failure. On the other hand, certain chemical reactions are desirable.

Other materials such as zirconium and niobium in solid solution may be deliberately incorporated in the fuel to alter the properties to those needed for the reactor design. Also, it is generally advantageous for some of the products of the nuclear reaction to remain in solid solution in the fuel, rather than accumulating as separate phases.

FUEL MATERIALS   Plant Materials

The physical properties of the fuel material are primarily of interest in ensuring its integrity during the manufacturing process. Nevertheless they must be considered in assessments of the integrity of the core under operating conditions, or the conditions of hypothetical accidents. The physical and mechanical properties should also permit economical manufacturing. The fuel material should have a low coefficient of expansion.

It is not possible to fabricate typical refractory ceramics to 100% of their theoretical density. Therefore, methods of controlling the porosity of the final product must be considered. The role of this initial porosity as sites for fission gas, as well as its effects on thermal conductivity and mechanical strength, is a significant factor in the design.

Summary

The important information in this chapter is summarized below.

Fuel Materials Summary

- Radioactive materials suitable for fission by thermal neutrons and used as reactor fuel include:

    ^{233}U and ^{235}U
    ^{239}Pu and ^{241}Pu

- Considerations in selecting fuel material are:

    High thermal conductivity so that high power can be attained without excessive fuel temperature gradients

    Resistance to radiation damage so that physical properties are not degraded

    Chemical stability with respect to coolant in case of cladding failure

    Physical and mechanical properties that permit economical fabrication

---

Plant Materials   CLADDING AND REFLECTORS

CLADDING AND REFLECTORS

Nuclear fuels require surface protection to retain fission products and minimize corrosion. Also, pelletized fuel requires a tubular container to hold the pellets in the required physical configuration. The requirements for cladding material to serve these different purposes will vary with the type of reactor; however, some general characteristics can be noted. This chapter will discuss the general characteristics associated with cladding and reflectors.

EO 1.5   **STATE the four major characteristics necessary in a material used for fuel cladding.**

EO 1.6   **IDENTIFY the four materials suitable for use as fuel cladding material and their applications.**

EO 1.7   **STATE the purpose of a reflector.**

EO 1.8   **LIST the five essential requirements for reflector material in a thermal reactor.**

Cladding

Cladding is used to provide surface protection for retaining fission products and minimizing corrosion. Cladding is also used to contain pelletized fuel to provide the required physical configuration.

Mechanical properties, such as ductility, impact strength, tensile strength, and creep, must be adequate for the operating conditions of the reactor core. Ease of fabrication is also important. It is desirable that ordinary fabrication procedures be applicable in fabricating the desired shape. The cladding must have a high corrosion resistance to its operating environment. It must have a high melting temperature to withstand abnormal operating conditions such as high temperature transients. Thermal conductivity should be high to minimize thermal stresses arising from temperature differences, and the coefficient of expansion should be low or well-matched with that of other materials. The cladding material should not be susceptible to radiation damage.

The nuclear properties of fuel cladding material must also be satisfactory. For thermal reactors, it is important that the material have a reasonably small absorption cross section for neutrons. Only four elements and their alloys have low thermal-neutron absorption cross sections and reasonably high melting points: aluminum, beryllium, magnesium, and zirconium. Of these, aluminum, magnesium, and zirconium are or have been utilized in fuel-element cladding.

Aluminum, such as the 1100 type, which is relatively pure (greater than 99%), has been used in low power, water-cooled research, training, and materials testing reactors in which the operating temperatures are below 100°C. Magnesium, in the form of the alloy magnox, serves as cladding for the uranium metal fuel in carbon-dioxide cooled, graphite-moderated power reactors in the United Kingdom. The alloy zircaloy, whose major constituent is zirconium, is widely used as the fuel-rod cladding in water-cooled power reactors. The alloys in common use as cladding material are zircaloy-2 and zircaloy-4, both of which have mechanical properties and corrosion resistance superior to those of zirconium itself. Although beryllium is suitable for use as cladding, it is not used due to its high cost and poor mechanical properties.

The choice of cladding material for fast reactors is less dependent upon the neutron absorption cross section than for thermal reactors. The essential requirements for these materials are high melting point, retention of satisfactory physical and mechanical properties, a low swelling rate when irradiated by large fluences of fast neutrons, and good corrosion resistance, especially to molten sodium. At present, stainless steel is the preferred fuel cladding material for sodium-cooled fast breeder reactors (LMFBRs). For such reactors, the capture cross section is not as important as for thermal neutron reactors.

In 1977 the Carter Administration deferred indefinitely the reprocessing of nuclear fuels from commercial power reactors. This led the electric utility industry to conduct research on high-burnup fuels and programs that would allow an increase in the length of time that the fuel rods remain in the reactors. High integrity and performance of fuel cladding will become even more important as these high-burnup fuel rods are designed and programs for extended burnup of nuclear fuels are placed into operation.

Reflector Materials

A *reflector* gets its name from the fact that neutrons leaving the reactor core hit the reflector and are returned to the core. The primary consideration for selecting a reflector material is its nuclear properties. The essential requirements for reflector material used in a thermal reactor are:

- Low macroscopic absorption (or capture) cross section to minimize loss of neutrons

- High macroscopic scattering cross section to minimize the distance between scatters

- High logarithmic energy decrement to maximize the energy loss per collision due to low mass number

- Temperature stability

- Radiation stability

Plant Materials   CLADDING AND REFLECTORS

In the case of a fast reactor, neutron thermalization is not desirable, and the reflector will consist of a dense element of high mass number.

Materials that have been used as reflectors include pure water, heavy water (deuterium oxide), beryllium (as metal or oxide), carbon (graphite), and zirconium hydride. The selection of which material to use is based largely on the nuclear considerations given above and the essential neuronic properties of the materials. Most power reactors use water as both the moderator and reflector, as well as the coolant. Graphite has been used extensively as moderator and reflector for thermal reactors. Beryllium is superior to graphite as a moderator and reflector material but, because of its high cost and poor mechanical properties, it has little prospect of being used to any extent. Beryllium has been used in a few instances such as test reactors, but is not used in any power reactors. Reactors using heavy water as the moderator-reflector have the advantage of being able to operate satisfactorily with natural uranium as the fuel material; enriched uranium is then not required. Zirconium hydride serves as the moderator in the Training, Research, Isotopes, General Atomic (TRIGA) reactor. The zirconium hydride is incorporated with enriched uranium metal in the fuel elements.

CLADDING AND REFLECTORS · Plant Materials

Summary

The important information in this chapter is summarized below.

Cladding and Reflectors Summary

- Major characteristics required for cladding material:

    Mechanical properties such as ductility, impact strength, tensile strength, creep, and ease of fabrication

    Physical properties include high corrosion resistance and high melting temperature

    High thermal conductivity

    Nuclear properties such as small absorption cross section

- Four materials suitable for cladding:

    Aluminum is used for low power, water-cooled research, training, and materials test reactors in which temperatures are below 100°C.

    Magnesium is used for uranium metal fuel in carbon-dioxide cooled, graphite-moderated power reactors in United Kingdom.

    Zirconium is used for fuel-rod cladding in water-cooled power reactors.

    Beryllium is suitable for use as cladding but is not used as such due to its high cost and poor mechanical properties. It is, however, used as a reflector in some test reactors.

- Reflectors are used to return neutrons leaving the reactor core back to the core.

- Essential requirements for reflectors include.
    Low macroscopic absorption cross section to minimize loss of neutrons
    High macroscopic scattering cross section
    High logarithmic energy decrement due to low mass number
    Temperature stability
    Radiation stability

CONTROL MATERIALS

Four general methods have been used or proposed for changing the power or neutron flux in a nuclear reactor; each involves the temporary addition or removal of (a) fuel, (b) moderator, (c) reflector, or (d) a neutron absorber or poison. This chapter discusses the materials used as poisons in a reactor plant.

EO 1.9   STATE the five common poisons used as control rod material.

EO 1.10   IDENTIFY the advantage(s) and/or disadvantage(s) of the five common poisons used as control rod material.

Overview of Poisons

The most commonly used method to control the nuclear reaction, especially in power reactors, is the insertion or withdrawal of control rods made out of materials (*poisons*) having a large cross section for the absorption of neutrons. The most widely-used poisons are hafnium, silver, indium, cadmium, and boron. These materials will be briefly discussed below.

Hafnium

Because of its neuronic, mechanical, and physical properties, hafnium is an excellent control material for water-cooled, water-moderated reactors. It is found together with zirconium, and the process that produces pure zirconium produces hafnium as a by-product. Hafnium is resistant to corrosion by high-temperature water, has adequate mechanical strength, and can be readily fabricated. Hafnium consists of four isotopes, each of which has appreciable neutron absorption cross sections. The capture of neutrons by the isotope hafnium-177 leads to the formation of hafnium-178; the latter forms hafnium-179, which leads to hafnium-180. The first three have large resonance-capture cross sections, and hafnium-180 has a moderately large cross section. Thus, the element hafnium in its natural form has a long, useful lifetime as a neutron absorber. Because of the limited availability and high cost of hafnium, its use as a control material in civilian power reactors has been restricted.

Silver-Indium-Cadmium Alloys

By alloying cadmium, which has a thermal-absorption cross section of 2450 barns, with silver and indium, which have high resonance absorption, a highly-effective neutron absorber is produced.

The control effectiveness of such alloys in water-moderated reactors can approach that of hafnium and is the control material commonly used in pressurized-water reactors. The alloys (generally 80% silver, 15% indium, 5% cadmium) can be readily fabricated and have adequate strength at water-reactor temperatures. The control material is enclosed in a stainless steel tube to protect it from corrosion by the high-temperature water.

Boron-Containing Materials

Boron is a useful control material for thermal (and other) reactors. The very high thermal-absorption cross section of ^{10}B (boron-10) and the low cost of boron has led to wide use of boron-containing materials in control rods and burnable poisons for thermal reactors. The absorption cross section of boron is large over a considerable range of neutron energies, making it suitable for not only control materials but also for neutron shielding.

Boron is nonmetallic and is not suitable for control rod use in its pure form. For reactor use, it is generally incorporated into a metallic material. Two of such composite materials are described below.

Stainless-steel alloys or dispersions with boron have been employed to some extent in reactor control. The performance of boron-stainless-steel materials is limited because of the ^{10}B (n,α) reaction. The absorption reaction is one of transmutation, ^{10}B + ^{1}n $\rightarrow$ ^{7}Li + $^{4}\alpha$, with the α-particle produced becoming a helium atom. The production of atoms having about twice the volume of the original atoms leads to severe swelling, hence these materials have not been used as control rods in commercial power reactors.

The refractory compound boron carbide (B$_4$C) has been used as a control material either alone or as a dispersion in aluminum (boral). These materials suffer from burnup limitation. The preferred control rod material for boiling-water reactors is boron carbide. Long stainless-steel tubes containing the powdered boron carbide combined into assemblies with cruciform cross sections make up the control rods. Control rods of this nature have been used in PWRs, BWRs, and HTGRs and have been proposed for use in fast breeder reactors employing oxide fuels. Because of its ability to withstand high temperatures, boron carbide (possibly mixed with graphite) will probably be the control material in future gas-cooled reactors operating at high temperatures.

In addition to its use in control elements, boron is widely used in PWRs for control of reactivity changes over core lifetime by dissolving boric acid in the coolant. When this scheme is used, the movable control elements have a reactivity worth sufficient to go from full power at operating temperature to zero power at operating temperature. At the beginning of life, enough boric acid is added to the coolant to allow the reactor to be just critical with all rods nearly completely withdrawn. As fuel burnup takes place through power operation, the boric acid concentration in the coolant is reduced to maintain criticality. If a cold shutdown is required, additional boric acid is added to compensate for the reactivity added as the moderator cools. This method is generally referred to as chemical shim control.

Boron may also be used as a burnable poison to compensate for the change in reactivity with lifetime. In this scheme, a small amount of boron is incorporated into the fuel or special burnable poison rods to reduce the beginning-of-life reactivity. Burnup of the poison causes a reactivity increase that partially compensates for the decrease in reactivity due to fuel burnup and accumulation of fission products. Difficulties have generally been encountered when boron is incorporated directly with the fuel, and most applications have used separate burnable poison rods.

Summary

The important information in this chapter is summarized below.

Control Materials Summary

- Hafnium

    Advantages: Excellent control for water-cooled, water-moderated reactors due to neutronic, mechanical, and physical properties.

    Disadvantages: Limited availability and high cost.

- Silver-Indium-Cadmium Alloys

    Advantages: Highly effective neutron absorber.

    Control effectiveness in water-moderated reactors is close to hafnium. Used in pressurized-water reactors.

    Easily fabricated and adequate strength

    Disadvantages: Must be enclosed in stainless steel tube to protect it from corrosion.

- Boron

    Advantages: Very high thermal-absorption cross-section and low cost.

    Commonly used in thermal reactors for control rods and burnable poison.

    Disadvantages: Nonmetallic thus must be incorporated into a metallic material for use as control rod.

SHIELDING MATERIALS

In the reactor plant, the principle source of radiation comes from the reactor core. Attenuation of this radiation is performed by shielding materials located around the core. This chapter discusses the various materials used in a reactor plant for shielding.

EO 1.11   DESCRIBE the requirements of a material used to shield against the following types of radiation:

    a.   Beta   c.   High energy neutrons
    b.   Gamma   d.   Low energy neutrons

Overview

Shielding design is relatively straightforward depending upon the type of radiation (gamma, neutron, alpha, beta). For example, when considering the reactor core, it is first necessary to slow down the fast neutrons (those not directly absorbed) coming from the core to thermal energy by utilizing appropriate neutron attenuating shielding materials that are properly arranged. This slowing down process is mostly caused by collisions that slow the neutrons to thermal energy. The thermal neutrons are then absorbed by the shielding material. All of the gamma rays in the system, both the gamma rays leaving the core and the gamma rays produced by neutron interactions within the shielding material have to be attenuated to appropriate levels by utilizing gamma ray shielding materials that are also properly arranged. The design of these radiation shields and those used to attenuate radiation from any radioactive source depend upon the location, the intensity, and the energy distribution of the radiation sources, and the permissible radiation levels at positions away from these sources. In this chapter, we will discuss the materials used to attenuate neutron, gamma, beta, and alpha radiation.

Neutron Radiation

The shielding of neutrons introduces many complications because of the wide range of energy that must be considered. At low energies (less than 0.1 MeV), low mass number materials, such as hydrogen in H_2O, are best for slowing down neutrons. At these energies, the cross section for interaction with hydrogen is high (approximately 20 barns), and the energy loss in a collision is high. Materials containing hydrogen are known as hydrogenous material, and their value as a neutron shield is determined by their hydrogen content. Water ranks high and is probably the best neutron shield material with the advantage of low cost, although it is a poor absorber of gamma radiation.

Water also provides a ready means for removing the heat generated by radiation absorption. At higher energies (10 MeV), the cross section for interaction with hydrogen (1 barn) is not as effective in slowing down neutrons. To offset this decrease in cross section with increased neutron energy, materials with good inelastic scattering properties, such as iron, are used. These materials cause a large change in neutron energy after collision for high energy neutrons but have little effect on neutrons at lower energy, below 0.1 MeV.

Iron, as carbon steel or stainless steel, has been commonly used as the material for thermal shields. Such shields can absorb a considerable proportion of the energy of fast neutrons and gamma rays escaping from the reactor core. By making shields composed of iron and water, it is possible to utilize the properties of both of these materials. PWRs utilize two or three layers of steel with water between them as a very effective shield for both neutrons and gamma rays. The interaction (inelastic scattering) of high energy neutrons occurs mostly with iron, which degrades the neutron to a much lower energy, where the water is more effective for slowing down (elastic scattering) neutrons. Once the neutron is slowed down to thermal energy, it diffuses through the shield medium for a small distance and is captured by the shielding material, resulting in a neutron-gamma (n,γ) reaction. These gamma rays represent a secondary source of radiation.

Iron turnings or punchings and iron oxide have been incorporated into heavy concrete for shielding purposes also. Concrete with seven weight percent or greater of water appears to be adequate for neutron attenuation. However, an increase in the water content has the disadvantage of decreasing both the density and structural strength of ordinary concrete. With heavy concretes, a given amount of attenuation of both neutrons and gamma rays can be achieved by means of a thinner shield than is possible with ordinary concrete. Various kinds of heavy concretes used for shielding include barytes concrete, iron concrete, and ferrophosphorus concrete with various modified concretes and related mixtures. Boron compounds (for example, the mineral colemanite) have also been added to concretes to increase the probability of neutron capture without high-energy gamma-ray production.

Boron has been included as a neutron absorber in various materials in addition to concrete. For example, borated graphite, a mixture of elemental boron and graphite, has been used in fast-reactor shields. Boral, consisting of boron carbide (B_4C) and aluminum, and epoxy resins and resin-impregnated wood laminates incorporating boron have been used for local shielding purposes. Boron has also been added to steel for shield structures to reduce secondary gamma-ray production. In special situations, where a shield has consisted of a heavy metal and water, it has been beneficial to add a soluble boron compound to the water.

Gamma Radiation

Gamma radiation is the most difficult to shield against and, therefore, presents the biggest problem in the reactor plant. The penetrating power of the gamma is due, in part, to the fact that it has no charge or mass. Therefore, it does not interact as frequently as do the other types of radiation per given material.

SHIELDING MATERIALS   Plant Materials

Gamma rays are attenuated by processes which are functions of atomic number and mass (that is they all involve interactions near the nucleus or interactions with the electrons around the nucleus). Gamma shielding is therefore more effectively performed by materials with high atomic mass number and high density. One such material is lead. Lead is dense and has about 82 electrons for each nucleus. Thus, a gamma would interact more times in passing through eight inches of lead then passing through the same thickness of a lighter material, such as water. As the gamma interacts with the shielding material, it loses energy and eventually disappears. Lead and lead alloys have been used to some extent in nuclear reactor shields and have an added advantage of ease of fabrication. Because of its low melting point, lead can be used only where the temperatures do not exceed its melting point.

Iron, although a medium weight element, also functions well as a gamma attenuator. For gamma rays with energies of 2 MeV, roughly the same mass of iron as of lead is required to remove a specific fraction of the radiation. At higher and lower energies, however, the mass-attenuation efficiency of lead is appreciably greater than that of iron. In many cases, the selection of iron is based on structural, temperature, and economic considerations.

Water is a poor material for shielding gamma rays; however, large amounts will serve to attenuate gamma radiation.

Concrete, as discussed previously, is also a good attenuator of gamma rays and is superior to water. This is mainly a result of the presence of moderately high mass number elements, such as calcium and silicon. As a general shield material, there is much to recommend about concrete; it is strong, inexpensive, and adaptable to both block and monolithic types of construction.

Alpha and Beta Radiation

Alpha particles, being the largest particles of radiation and having a +2 charge, interact with matter more readily than other types of radiation. Each interaction results in a loss of energy. This is why the alpha has the shortest range of all the types of radiation. Alpha particles generally are stopped by a thin sheet of paper. As a comparison, a 4 MeV alpha particle will travel about 1 inch in air, whereas a 4 MeV beta particle will travel about 630 inches in air. Because it deposits all of its energy in a very small area, the alpha particle travels only a short distance.

The beta particle is more penetrating than the alpha. However, because of the -1 charge, the beta particle interacts more readily than a non-charged particle. For this reason, it is less penetrating than uncharged types of radiation such as the gamma or neutron. The beta particle can generally be stopped by a sheet of aluminum. Because the beta travels farther than the alpha, it deposits its energy over a greater area and is, therefore, less harmful than the alpha if taken internally. All materials described under neutron and gamma radiation are also effective at attenuating beta radiation.

Since alpha and beta particles can be easily shielded against, they do not present a major problem in the nuclear reactor plant.

Summary

The important information in this chapter is summarized below.

Shielding Materials Summary

- Neutron Radiation

    Low mass number and high cross section (preferably hydrogenous material) for low energies. Water ranks high due to advantage of low cost, ready means for removing heat.

    Good inelastic scattering properties (high energies). Iron is used due to the large change in neutron energy after collision but it has little effect on lower energy neutrons.

- Gamma Radiation

    High atomic mass number and high density are required to attenuate γ radiation. Lead has advantage of ease of fabrication. The disadvantage of lead is its low melting point. Iron is used for higher and lower energies. Iron is selected based on structural, temperature, and economic considerations. Water can be used but requires large amounts because water is a poor absorber of gamma radiation. Concrete is a good gamma attenuator as a general shield material. Concrete is strong, inexpensive, and adaptable to different types of construction.

- Alpha and Beta Radiation

    No particular shielding material is required to guard against alphas and betas.

NUCLEAR REACTOR CORE PROBLEMS   Plant Materials

NUCLEAR REACTOR CORE PROBLEMS

Material problems in a nuclear reactor plant can be grouped into at least two categories, one concerning the nuclear reactor core and one that will apply to all plant materials. This chapter discusses specific material problems associated with the reactor that include pellet-cladding interaction, fuel densification, fuel-cladding embrittlement, and effects on fuel due to inclusion and core burnup.

EO 1.12   STATE nuclear reactor core problems and causes associated with the following:

   a.   Pellet-cladding interaction
   b.   Fuel densification
   c.   Fuel cladding embrittlement
   d.   Fuel burnup and fission product swelling

EO 1.13   STATE measures taken to counteract or minimize the effects of the following:

   a.   Pellet-cladding interaction
   b.   Fuel densification
   c.   Fuel cladding embrittlement
   d.   Fission product swelling of fuel elements

Fuel Pellet-Cladding Interaction

Fuel pellet-cladding interaction (PCI) may lead to cladding failure and subsequent release of fission products into the reactor coolant. PCI appears to be a complex phenomenon that tends to occur under power ramping conditions. Expansion of the fuel pellets due to high internal temperatures, cracking due to thermal stresses, and irradiation-induced swelling may lead to contact of the fuel with the cladding. Thermal, chemical, and mechanical interactions may then occur that, if not appropriately accounted for in the design, may lead to cladding failure. Design features to counteract PCI include the following.

   a. an increase in the cladding thickness

   b. an increase in the cladding-pellet gap, with pressurization to prevent cladding collapse

   c. the introduction of a layer of graphite or other lubricant between the fuel and the cladding

Operational limitations such as rate of power increase and power for a given power ramp rate are imposed to lessen the effect of PCI. PCI appears to be more likely to occur during initial power increase and can be very costly if cladding failure occurs.

Fuel Densification

Some uranium dioxide (UO_2) fuels have exhibited densification, the reverse of swelling, as a result of irradiation. Such behavior can cause the fuel material to contract and lead to irregularities in the thermal power generation. The changes in fuel pellet dimensions have been small because the changes are localized in the central region of the pellet and are somewhat masked by other physical changes that occur at high temperatures during the early part of the fuel cycle.

Fuel densification increases the percent of theoretical density of UO_2 pellets from a range of 90% to 95% to a range of 97% to 98%. Densification apparently arises from the elimination of small pores in the UO_2 pellets. As densification takes place, axial and radial shrinkage of the fuel pellet results and a 3.66 m column of fuel pellets can decrease in length by as much as 7.5 cm or more. As the column settles, mechanical interaction between the cladding and the pellet may occur, preventing the settling of the pellet and those above it on the column below. Once the gap has been produced, outside water pressure can flatten the cladding in the gap region, resulting in a flux spike. Because the thermal expansion of UO_2 is greater than that of zircaloy, and the thermal response time for the fuel during power change is shorter than that of the cladding, the pellet temperature changes more quickly than the temperature of the cladding during a power change. If creep (slow deformation) of the cladding has diminished the gap between the cladding and the fuel pellets, it is possible for the difference in thermal expansion to cause stresses exceeding the yield for the cladding material. Because irradiation reduces cladding ductility, the differential expansion may lead to cladding failure. The process of fuel densification is complete within 200 hours of reactor operation.

The problems of cladding collapse resulting from fuel densification and cladding creep have occurred mainly with unpressurized fuel rods in PWRs. To reduce the cladding creep sufficiently to prevent the formation of fuel column gaps and subsequent tubing collapse, the following methods have been successful: pressurizing the fuel rods with helium to pressures of 200 psig to 400 psig; and increasing fuel pellet density by sintering (bonded mass of metal particles shaped and partially fused by pressure and heating below the melting point) the material in a manner leading to a higher initial density and a stabilized pore microstructure.

There are three principle effects associated with fuel densification that must be evaluated for reactors in all modes of operation.

    a. an increase in the linear heat generation rate by an amount directly proportional to the decrease in pellet length

    b. an increased local neutron flux and a local power spike in the axial gaps in the fuel column

c. a decrease in the clearance gap heat conductance between the pellets and the cladding. This decrease in heat transmission capability will increase the energy stored in the fuel pellet and will cause an increased fuel temperature.

To minimize the effects of fuel densification, plant procedures limit the maximum permissible rate at which power may be increased to ensure that the temperature will not exceed 1200°C during a loss of coolant accident. This allows the fuel pellets to shift slowly, with less chance of becoming jammed during the densification process, which in turn reduces the chance of cladding failure.

Fuel Cladding Embrittlement

Corrosion of zircaloy in water results in the release of hydrogen. A portion of the hydrogen released, ranging from about 5% to 20%, diffuses through the oxide layer and into the metal. This causes embrittlement of the base metal that can lead to cladding failure. The mechanism of hydrogen embrittlement is discussed in Module 2, Properties of Metals. The zirconium alloy zircaloy-2, which has been used extensively as a fuel-rod cladding, is subject to hydrogen embrittlement, especially in the vicinity of surface defects. The alloy zircaloy-4 is, however, less susceptible to embrittlement. As with metals in general, irradiation decreases the ductility and increases the embrittlement of zirconium and the zircaloys. The magnitude of the radiation effect depends upon the neutron spectrum, fluence, temperature, and microstructure (or texture) of the material. Different fabrication processes yield products with different textures; therefore, the radiation embrittlement of zircaloy is dependent on its fabrication history.

Irradiation at high temperatures can lead to brittle fracture of stainless steels used as cladding in fast liquid metal breeder reactors. The effects of irradiation on metals is discussed in more detail in a later chapter of this module.

Effects on Fuel Due to Swelling and Core Burnup

One of the requirements of a good fuel is to be resistant to radiation damage that can lead to dimensional changes (for example, by swelling, cracking, or creep). Early reactors and some older gas-cooled reactors used unalloyed uranium as the fuel. When unalloyed uranium is irradiated, dimensional changes occur that present drawbacks to its use as a fuel. The effects are of two types: 1) dimensional instability without appreciable change in density observed at temperatures below about 450°C, and 2) swelling, accompanied by a decrease in density, which becomes important above 450°C. Other reactors use ceramic fuels, with uranium dioxide being the most common, have the advantages of high-temperature stability and adequate resistance to radiation. Uranium dioxide (UO_2) has the ability to retain a large proportion of the fission gases, provided the temperature does not exceed about 1000°C. Other oxide fuels have similar qualities.

Even though fission product swelling is less with oxide fuels, this irradiation-induced volume increase has been observed in UO_2 and mixed-oxide fuels for a number of years. This swelling of the fuel has generally been attributed to both gaseous fission-product bubble formation and the accumulation of solid fission products. Swelling can cause excessive pressure on the cladding, which could lead to fuel element cladding failure. Swelling also becomes a consideration on the lifetime of the fuel element by helping to determine the physical and mechanical changes resulting from irradiation and high temperature in the fuel and the cladding. Fuel element life or core burnup, which indicates the useful lifetime of the fuel in a reactor, is also determined by the decrease in reactivity due to the decrease in fissile material and the accumulation of fission-product poisons. Under operating conditions, fuel pellets undergo marked structural changes as a result of the high internal temperatures and the large temperature gradients. Thermal stresses lead to radial cracks and grain structure changes. These structural changes tend to increase with the specific power and burnup of the fuel.

Summary

The important information in this chapter is summarized below.

Nuclear Reactor Core Problems Summary

- Fuel Pellet-Cladding Interaction (PCI)

    PCI may lead to cladding failure and subsequent release of fission products into the reactor coolant.

    Expansion of the fuel pellets due to high internal temperatures, cracking due to thermal stresses, and irradiation-induced swelling may lead to contact of the fuel with the cladding.

    Design features to counteract PCI include:

    - An increase in the cladding thickness

    - An increase in the clad-pellet gap, with pressurization to obviate cladding collapse

    - The introduction of a layer of graphite or other lubricant between the fuel and the cladding

    Operational limitations to reduce PCI

    - Plant procedures limit the maximum permissible rate at which power may be increased to lessen the effect of PCI.

Nuclear Reactor Core Problems Summary (Cont.)

- Fuel Densification

    Densification, which is the reverse of swelling, is a result of irradiation. Such behavior can cause the fuel material to contract and lead to irregularities in the thermal power generation.

    Three principle effects:

    An increase in the linear heat generation rate by an amount directly proportional to the decrease in pellet length

    An increased local neutron flux and a local power spike in the axial gaps in the fuel column

    A decrease in the clearance gap heat conductance between the pellets and the cladding. This decrease in heat transmission capability will increase the energy stored in the fuel pellet and will cause an increased fuel temperature.

    To minimize these effects on power plant operation, limits are established on the power level rate of change and the maximum cladding temperature (1200°C) allowable during a loss of coolant accident.

- Fuel Cladding Embrittlement

    Embrittlement is caused by hydrogen diffusing into the metal. Cladding embrittlement can lead to cladding failure.

    Zircaloy-4 and different fabrication processes are used to minimize the effect of hydrogen embrittlement.

- Fuel Burnup and Fission Product Swelling

    High fuel burnup rate can cause the reactor to be refueled earlier than designed. Swelling can cause excessive pressure on the cladding, which could lead to fuel element cladding failure.

    Operational maximum and minimum coolant flow limitations help prevent extensive fuel element damage.

PLANT MATERIAL PROBLEMS

Material problems in a nuclear reactor plant can be grouped into two categories, one concerning the nuclear reactor core and one that will apply to all plant materials. This chapter discusses specific material problems associated with fatigue failure, work hardening, mechanical forces applied to materials, stress, and strain.

EO 1.14   DEFINE the following terms:

    a.   Fatigue failure
    b.   Work hardening
    c.   Creep

EO 1.15   STATE measures taken to counteract or minimize the effects of the following:

    a.   Fatigue failure
    b.   Work hardening
    c.   Creep

Fatigue Failure

The majority of engineering failures are caused by fatigue. *Fatigue failure* is defined as the tendency of a material to fracture by means of progressive brittle cracking under repeated alternating or cyclic stresses of an intensity considerably below the normal strength. Although the fracture is of a brittle type, it may take some time to propagate, depending on both the intensity and frequency of the stress cycles. Nevertheless, there is very little, if any, warning before failure if the crack is not noticed. The number of cycles required to cause fatigue failure at a particular peak stress is generally quite large, but it decreases as the stress is increased. For some mild steels, cyclical stresses can be continued indefinitely provided the peak stress (sometimes called fatigue strength) is below the endurance limit value.

A good example of fatigue failure is breaking a thin steel rod or wire with your hands after bending it back and forth several times in the same place. Another example is an unbalanced pump impeller resulting in vibrations that can cause fatigue failure.

The type of fatigue of most concern in nuclear power plants is thermal fatigue. Thermal fatigue can arise from thermal stresses produced by cyclic changes in temperature. Large components like the pressurizer, reactor vessel, and reactor system piping are subject to cyclic stresses caused by temperature variations during reactor startup, change in power level, and shutdown.

Fundamental requirements during design and manufacturing for avoiding fatigue failure are different for different cases. For a pressurizer, the load variations are fairly low, but the cycle frequency is high; therefore, a steel of high fatigue strength and of high ultimate tensile strength is desirable. The reactor pressure vessel and piping, by contrast, are subjected to large load variations, but the cycle frequency is low; therefore, high ductility is the main requirement for the steel. Thermal sleeves are used in some cases, such as spray nozzles and surge lines, to minimize thermal stresses. Although the primary cause of the phenomenon of fatigue failure is not well known, it apparently arises from the initial formation of a small crack resulting from a defect or microscopic slip in the metal grains. The crack propagates slowly at first and then more rapidly when the local stress is increased due to a decrease in the load-bearing cross section. The metal then fractures. Fatigue failure can be initiated by microscopic cracks and notches, and even by grinding and machining marks on the surface; therefore, such defects must be avoided in materials subjected to cyclic stresses (or strains). These defects also favor brittle fracture, which is discussed in detail in Module 4, Brittle Fracture.

Plant operations are performed in a controlled manner to mitigate the effects of cyclic stress. Heatup and cooldown limitations, pressure limitations, and pump operating curves are all used to minimize cyclic stress. In some cases, cycle logs may be kept on various pieces of equipment. This allows that piece of equipment to be replaced before fatigue failure can take place.

Work (Strain) Hardening

Work hardening is when a metal is strained beyond the yield point. An increasing stress is required to produce additional plastic deformation and the metal apparently becomes stronger and more difficult to deform.

Stress-strain curves are discussed in Module 2, Properties of Metals. If true stress is plotted against true strain, the rate of strain hardening tends to become almost uniform, that is, the curve becomes almost a straight line, as shown in Figure 1. The gradient of the straight part of the line is known as the strain hardening coefficient or work hardening coefficient, and is closely related to the shear modulus (about proportional). Therefore, a metal with a high shear modulus will have a high strain or work hardening coefficient (for example, molybdenum). Grain size will also influence strain hardening. A material with small grain size will strain harden more rapidly than the same material with a larger grain size. However, the effect only applies in the early stages of plastic deformation, and the influence disappears as the structure deforms and grain structure breaks down.

Work hardening is closely related to fatigue. In the example on fatigue given above, bending the thin steel rod becomes more difficult the farther the rod is bent. This is the result of work or strain hardening. Work hardening reduces ductility, which increases the chances of brittle failure.

Plant Materials   PLANT MATERIAL PROBLEMS

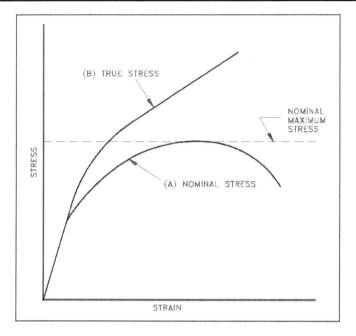

Figure 1 Nominal Stress-Strain Curve
vs True Stress-Strain Curve

Work hardening can also be used to treat material. Prior work hardening (cold working) causes the treated material to have an apparently higher yield stress. Therefore, the metal is strengthened.

Creep

At room temperature, structural materials develop the full strain they will exhibit as soon as a load is applied. This is not necessarily the case at high temperatures (for example, stainless steel above 1000°F or zircaloy above 500°F). At elevated temperatures and constant stress or load, many materials continue to deform at a slow rate. This behavior is called creep. At a constant stress and temperature, the rate of creep is approximately constant for a long period of time. After this period of time and after a certain amount of deformation, the rate of creep increases, and fracture soon follows. This is illustrated in Figure 2.

Initially, primary or transient creep occurs in Stage I. The creep rate, (the slope of the curve) is high at first, but it soon decreases. This is followed by secondary (or steady-state) creep in Stage II, when the creep rate is small and the strain increases very slowly with time. Eventually, in Stage III (tertiary or accelerating creep), the creep rate increases more rapidly and the strain may become so large that it results in failure.

PLANT MATERIAL PROBLEMS   Plant Materials

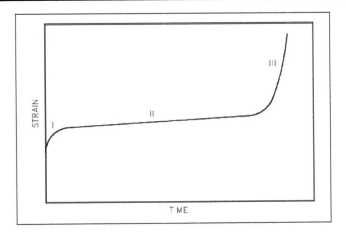

Figure 2 Successive Stages of Creep with Increasing Time

The rate of creep is highly dependent on both stress and temperature. With most of the engineering alloys used in construction at room temperature or lower, creep strain is so small at working loads that it can safely be ignored. It does not become significant until the stress intensity is approaching the fracture failure strength. However, as temperature rises creep becomes progressively more important and eventually supersedes fatigue as the likely criterion for failure. The temperature at which creep becomes important will vary with the material.

For safe operation, the total deformation due to creep must be well below the strain at which failure occurs. This can be done by staying well below the creep limit, which is defined as the stress to which a material can be subjected without the creep exceeding a specified amount after a given time at the operating temperature (for example, a creep rate of 0.01 in 100,000 hours at operating temperature). At the temperature at which high-pressure vessels and piping operate, the creep limit generally does not pose a limitation. On the other hand, it may be a drawback in connection with fuel element cladding. Zircaloy has a low creep limit, and zircaloy creep is a major consideration in fuel element design. For example, the zircaloy cladding of fuel elements in PWRs has suffered partial collapse caused by creep under the influence of high temperature and a high pressure load. Similarly, creep is a consideration at the temperatures that stainless-steel cladding encounters in gas-cooled reactors and fast reactors where the stainless-steel cladding temperature may exceed 540°C.

Plant Materials   PLANT MATERIAL PROBLEMS

Summary

The important information in this chapter is summarized below.

Plant Material Problems Summary

- Fatigue Failure

    Thermal fatigue is the fatigue type of most concern. Thermal fatigue results from thermal stresses produced by cyclic changes in temperature.

    Fundamental requirements during design and manufacturing are used to avoid fatigue failure.

    Plant operations are performed in a controlled manner to mitigate cyclic stress. Heatup and cooldown limitations, pressure limitations, and pump operating curves are also used to minimize cyclic stress.

- Work Hardening

    Work hardening has the effect of reducing ductility, which increases the chances of brittle fracture.

    Prior work hardening causes the treated material to have an apparently higher yield stress; therefore, the metal is strengthened.

- Creep

    Creep is the result of materials deforming when undergoing elevated temperatures and constant stress. Creep becomes a problem when the stress intensity is approaching the fracture failure strength. If the creep rate increases rapidly, the strain becomes so large that it could result in failure. The creep rate is controlled by minimizing the stress and temperature of a material.

ATOMIC DISPLACEMENT DUE TO IRRADIATION

The effects of radiation on plant materials depend on both the type of radiation and the type of material. This chapter discusses atomic displacements resulting from the various types of radiation.

EO 1.16　　STATE how the following types of radiation interact with metals.

　　a.　Gamma　　　d.　Fast neutron
　　b.　Alpha　　　　e.　Slow neutron
　　c.　Beta

EO 1.17　　DEFINE the following terms:

　　a.　Knock-on
　　b.　Vacancy
　　c.　Interstitial

Overview

Ionization and excitation of electrons in metals is produced by beta and gamma radiation. The ionization and excitation dissipates much of the energy of heavier charged particles and does very little damage. This is because electrons are relatively free to move and are soon replaced. The net effect of beta and gamma radiation on metal is to generate a small amount of heat.

Heavier particles, such as protons, α-particles, fast neutrons, and fission fragments, will usually transfer sufficient energy through elastic or inelastic collisions to remove nuclei from their lattice (crystalline) positions. This addition of vacancies and interstitial atoms causes property changes in metals. This effect of nuclear radiation is sometimes referred to as *radiation damage*.

In materials other than metals in which chemical bonds are important to the nature of the material, the electronic interactions (ionizations) are important because they can break chemical bonds. This is important in materials such as organics. The breaking of chemical bonds can lead to both larger and smaller molecules depending on the repair mechanism.

In either case there are material property changes, and these changes tend to be greater for a given dose than for metals, because much more of the radiation energy goes into ionization energy than into nuclear collisions.

Atomic Displacements

If a target or struck nucleus gains about 25 eV of kinetic energy (25 eV to 30 eV for most metals) in a collision with a radiation particle (usually a fast neutron), the nucleus will be displaced from its equilibrium position in the crystal lattice, as shown in Figure 3.

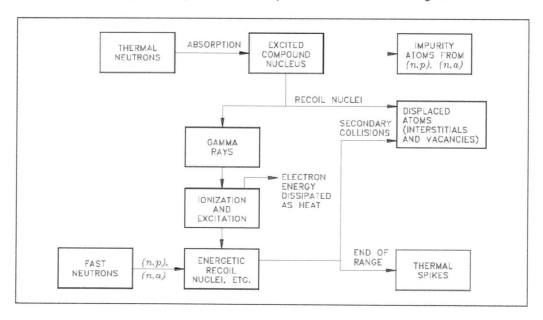

Figure 3 Thermal and Fast Neutrons Interactions with a Solid

The target nucleus (or recoiling atom) that is displaced is called a *knocked-on* nucleus or just a *knock-on* (or primary knock-on). When a metal atom is ejected from its crystal lattice the vacated site is called a *vacancy*. The amount of energy required to displace an atom is called *displacement energy*. The ejected atom will travel through the lattice causing ionization and heating. If the energy of the knock-on atom is large enough, it may in turn produce additional collisions and knock-ons. These knock-ons are referred to as secondary knock-ons. The process will continue until the displaced atom does not have sufficient energy to eject another atom from the crystal lattice. Therefore, a cascade of knock-on atoms will develop from the initial interaction of a high energy radiation particle with an atom in a solid.

This effect is especially important when the knock-on atom (or nucleus) is produced as the result of an elastic collision with a fast neutron (or other energetic heavy particle). The energy of the primary knock-on can then be quite high, and the cascade may be extensive. A single fast neutron in the greater than or equal to 1 MeV range can displace a few thousand atoms. Most of these displacements are temporary. At high temperatures, the number of permanently displaced atoms is smaller than the initial displacement.

During a lengthy irradiation (for large values of the neutron fluence), many of the displaced atoms will return to normal (stable) lattice sites (that is, partial annealing occurs spontaneously). The permanently displaced atoms may lose their energy and occupy positions other than normal crystal lattice sites (or nonequilibrium sites), thus becoming *interstitials*. The presence of interstitials and vacancies makes it more difficult for dislocations to move through the lattice. This increases the strength and reduces the ductility of a material.

At high energies, the primary knock-on (ion) will lose energy primarily by ionization and excitation interactions as it passes through the lattice, as shown in Figure 3. As the knock-on loses energy, it tends to pick up free electrons which effectively reduces its charge. As a result, the principle mechanism for energy losses progressively changes from one of ionization and excitation at high energies to one of elastic collisions that produce secondary knock-ons or displacements. Generally, most elastic collisions between a knock-on and a nucleus occur at low kinetic energies below A keV, where A is the mass number of the knock-on. If the kinetic energy is greater than A keV, the probability is that the knock-on will lose much of its energy in causing ionization.

Summary

The important information in this chapter is summarized below.

Atomic Displacement Due To Irradiation Summary

- Beta and gamma radiation produce ionization and excitation of electrons, which does very little damage.

- Heavier particles, such as protons, α-particles, fast neutrons, and fission fragments, usually transfer energy through elastic or inelastic collisions to cause radiation damage. These particles in organic material break the chemical bonds, which will change the material's properties.

- Knock-on is a target nucleus (or recoiling atom) that is displaced.

- Vacancy is the vacated site when a metal atom is ejected from its crystal lattice.

- Interstitial is a permanently displaced atom that has lost its energy and is occupying a position other than its normal crystal lattice site.

THERMAL AND DISPLACEMENT SPIKES DUE TO IRRADIATION

Thermal and displacement spikes can cause distortion that is frozen as stress in the microscopic area. These spikes can cause a change in the material's properties.

EO 1.18   DEFINE the following terms:

   a.   Thermal spike
   b.   Displacement spike

EO 1.19   STATE the effect a large number of displacement spikes has on the properties of a metal.

Thermal Spikes

As mentioned previously, the knock-ons lose energy most readily when they have lower energies, because they are in the vicinity longer and therefore interact more strongly. A *thermal spike* occurs when radiation deposits energy in the form of a knock-on, which in turn, transfers its excess energy to the surrounding atoms in the form of vibrational energy (heat). Some of the distortion from the heating can be frozen as a stress in this microscopic area.

Displacement Spikes

A *displacement spike* occurs when many atoms in a small area are displaced by a knock-on (or cascade of knock-ons). A 1 MeV neutron may affect approximately 5000 atoms, making up one of these spikes. The presence of many displacement spikes will change the properties of the material being irradiated. A displacement spike contains large numbers of interstitials and lattice vacancies (referred to as Frenkel pairs or Frenkel defects when considered in pairs). The presence of large numbers of vacancies and interstitials in the lattice of a metal will generally increase hardness and decrease ductility. In many materials (for example, graphite, uranium metal) bulk volume increases occur.

Summary

The important information in this chapter is summarized below.

Thermal and Displacement Spikes
Due To Irradiation Summary

- Thermal spikes occur when radiation deposits energy in the form of a knock-on, which in turn, transfers its excess energy to the surrounding atoms in the form of vibrational energy (heat).

- Displacement spikes occur when many atoms in a small area are displaced by a knock-on.

- The presence of many displacement spikes changes the properties of the metal being irradiated, such as increasing hardness and decreasing ductility.

EFFECT DUE TO NEUTRON CAPTURE

Neutron radiation affects material because of neutrons being captured. This chapter discusses the effects that the neutrons being captured have on the material.

EO 1.20   **DESCRIBE** how the emission of radiation can cause dislocation of the atom emitting the radiation.

EO 1.21   **STATE** the two effects on a crystalline structure resulting from the capture of a neutron.

EO 1.22   **STATE** how thermal neutrons can produce atomic displacements.

Effect Due to Neutron Capture

The effects of neutrons on materials arise largely from the transfer of kinetic energy to atomic nuclei in one way or another. Thus, highly energetic recoil nuclei may be indirectly produced by the absorption of a neutron and the subsequent emission of a γ. As previously discussed, if the energy of the recoil nucleus is sufficient to permit it to be displaced from its normal (or equilibrium) position in the crystal lattice of a solid, physical changes of an essentially permanent nature will be observed. The effects of fast neutrons in disrupting (or damaging) the crystal lattice by displacement of atoms are discussed in the two previous chapters, "Atomic Displacement Due to Irradiation" and "Thermal and Displacement Spikes Due to Irradiation." This damage is commonly referred to as radiation damage. The absorption or capture of lower energy thermal neutrons can produce two effects.

    a.   introduction of an impurity atom (this is used in the electronics industry to uniformly dope semiconductors) due to the transmutation of the absorbing nucleus

    b.   atomic displacement caused by recoil atoms or knock-ons

As noted, the introduction of an impurity atom was discussed previously, and atomic displacement is the result of (n,p) and (n,α) reactions and (n,γ) reactions followed by radioactive decay. Thermal neutrons cannot produce atomic displacements directly, but they can do so indirectly as the result of radioactive capture (n,γ) and other neutron reactions or elastic scattering.

EFFECT DUE TO NEUTRON CAPTURE

Radioactive capture, or thermal neutron capture, produces many gamma rays (sometimes called photons) in the 5 MeV to 10 MeV energy range. When a gamma-ray photon is emitted by the excited compound nucleus formed by neutron capture, the residual atom suffers recoil (sometimes referred to as the shotgun effect). This recoil energy is often large enough to displace the atom from its equilibrium position and produce a cascade of displacements, or Frenkel defects, with a resultant property change of the material. The (n,γ) reaction with thermal neutrons can displace the atom since the gamma photon has momentum ($\frac{E_\gamma}{c}$), which means that the nucleus must have an equal and opposite momentum (conservation of momentum). E_γ is the gamma-ray (photon) energy, and c is the velocity of light. If the recoil atom has mass A, it will recoil with a velocity υ such that

$$\frac{E_\gamma}{c} = A\upsilon \qquad (5\text{-}1)$$

where all quantities are expressed in SI units. The recoil energy E_r is equal to $1/2\, A\upsilon^2$, so that

$$E_r = \frac{E_\gamma^2}{2Ac^2} \,. \qquad (5\text{-}2)$$

Upon converting the energies into MeV and A into atomic mass (or weight) units, the result is

$$E_r = 5.4 \times 10^{-4}\, \frac{E_\gamma^2}{A} \,. \qquad (5\text{-}3)$$

The maximum energy of a gamma ray accompanying a (n,γ) reaction is in the range between 6 MeV and 8 MeV. For an element of low atomic mass (about 10), the recoil energy could be 2 keV to 3 keV, which is much greater than the 25 eV necessary to displace an atom.

In a thermal reactor, in which the thermal neutron flux generally exceeds the fast neutron flux, the radiation damage caused by recoil from (n,γ) reactions may be of the same order as (or greater than) that due to the fast neutrons in a material having an appreciable radioactive capture cross section for thermal neutrons. Other neutron reactions (for example, (n,p), (n,γ)) will also produce recoil atoms, but these reactions are of little significance in thermal reactors. Thermal neutron capture effects are generally confined to the surface of the material because most captures occur there, but fast-neutron damage is likely to extend through most of the material.

Impurity atoms are produced by nuclear transmutations. Neutron capture in a reactor produces an isotope that may be unstable and produce an entirely new atom as it decays. For most metallic materials, long irradiations at high flux levels are necessary to produce significant property changes due to the building of impurities. However, a semiconductor such as germanium (Ge) may have large changes in conductivity due to the gallium and arsenic atoms that are introduced as the activated Ge isotopes decay. In stainless steel, trace amounts of boron undergo a (n,α) reaction that generates helium bubbles which lead to the deterioration of mechanical properties.

Physical Effects of Radiation

The general physical and mechanical effects of the irradiation of metals by fast neutrons and other high-energy particles are summarized in Table 1.

TABLE 1
General Effects of Fast-Neutron Irradiation on Metals

Property Increases	Property Decreases
Yield strength	Ductility
Tensile strength	Stress-rupture strength
NDT temperature	Density
Young's Modulus (slight)	Impact strength
Hardness	Thermal conductivity
High-temperature creep rate (during irradiation)	

For fast neutrons, the changes are usually undetectable below certain radiation levels (fluences below 10^{22} neutrons/m^2). With increasing radiation levels, the magnitude of the effects increases and may reach a limit at very large fluences. The effects listed in Table 1 are generally less significant at elevated temperatures for a given fluence and some defects can be removed by heating (annealing).

Both the yield strength and the tensile strength of a metal are increased by irradiation, as shown in Table 2, but the increase in yield strength is generally greater than the increase in tensile strength. At the same time, ductility is decreased by irradiation as shown in Figure 4, which is representative of the behavior of many metals, including steel and zircaloy. The accelerated decrease in the ductility of reactor vessels is due to the residual copper (Cu), phosphorous (P), and nickel (Ni) content in the vessel steel.

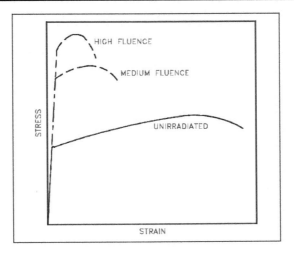

Figure 4 Qualitative Representation of Neutron Irradiation Effect on Many Metals

For stainless steel exposed to a thermal reactor fluence of 10^{21} neutrons/cm^2, the tensile properties show some increase in ultimate strength (tensile strength), an almost threefold gain in the yield strength, and a drop of about one third in ductility (elongation), as shown in Table 2.

The Nil-Ductility Transition (NDT) temperature, which is the temperature at which a given metal changes from ductile to brittle fracture, is often markedly increased by neutron irradiation. The increase in the NDT temperature is one of the most important effects of irradiation from the standpoint of nuclear power system design. For economic reasons, the large core pressure vessels of large power reactors have been constructed of low carbon steels.

The loss of ductility and increase in the NDT temperature of these vessels is a primary concern to reactor designers because of the increased chance of brittle fracture. Brittle fracture of a material is a failure occurring by crystal cleavage and accompanied by essentially no yielding. A brittle fracture of a pressure vessel resembles the shattering of glass. Since such a failure would be disastrous, it is necessary to understand the brittle fracture mechanism. During normal reactor operation, the pressure-vessel steel is subject to increasing fluence of fast neutrons and, as a result, the NDT temperature increases steadily. The NDT temperature is not likely to increase sufficiently to approach the temperature of the steel in the pressure vessel. However, as the reactor is being cooled down, the temperature of the vessel may drop below the NDT value while the reactor vessel is still pressurized. Brittle fracture might then occur.

TABLE 2
Effect of Fast-Neutron Irradiation on the Mechanical Properties of Metals

Material	Integrated Fast Flux (NVT)	Radiation Temperature (°C)	Tensile Strength (MPa)	Yield Strength (MPa)	Elongation (%)
Austenitic SS Type 304	0	------	576	235	65
	1.2×10^{21}	100	720	663	42
Low Carbon steel A-212 (.2%C)	0	------	517	276	25
	2.0×10^{19}	80	676	634	6
	1.0×10^{20}	80	800	752	4
	2.0×10^{19}	293	703	524	9
	2.0×10^{19}	404	579	293	14
Aluminum 6061-0	0	------	124	65	28.8
	1.0×10^{20}	66	257	177	22.4
Aluminum 6061-T6	0	------	310	265	17.5
	1.0×10^{20}	66	349	306	16.2
Zircaloy-2	0	------	276	155	13
	1.0×10^{20}	138	310	279	4

One of the areas of the reactor vessel that is of most concern is the beltline region. The Nuclear Regulatory Commission requires that a reactor vessel material surveillance program be conducted (in accordance with ASTM standards) in water-cooled power reactors. Specimens of steel used in the pressure vessel must be placed inside the vessel located near the inside vessel wall in the beltline region, so that the neutron flux received by the specimens approximates that received by the vessel inner surface, and the thermal environment is as close as possible to that of the vessel inner surface. The specimens are withdrawn at prescribed intervals during the reactor lifetime and are subjected to impact tests to determine new NDT temperatures. Figure 5 shows the increase in NDT temperature for a representative group of low carbon steel alloys irradiated at temperatures below 232°C. Many current reactors have core pressure vessel wall temperatures in the range of 200°C to 290°C, so that an increase in NDT is of very real concern.

Irradiation frequently decreases the density of a metal over a certain temperature range, so that a specimen exhibits an increase in volume or swelling. The swelling of stainless steel structural components and fuel rod cladding, resulting from fast neutron irradiation at the temperatures existing in fast reactors, is a matter of great concern in fast reactors. The swelling can cause changes in the dimensions of the coolant channels and also interfere with the free movement of control elements.

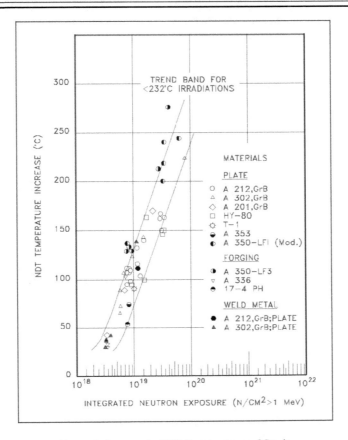

Figure 5 Increase in NDT Temperatures of Steels
from Irradiation Below 232°C

The generally accepted explanation of irradiation-induced swelling is based on the characteristics of interstitial loops and voids or vacancy loops. If the temperature is high enough to permit interstitials and vacancies, but not high enough to allow recombination, a relatively large (supersaturated) concentration of defects can be maintained under irradiation. Under these circumstances, the interstitials tend to agglomerate, or cluster, to form roughly circular two-dimensional disks, or platelets, commonly called interstitial loops. A dislocation loop is formed when the collapse (or readjustment) of adjacent atomic planes takes place. On the other hand, vacancies can agglomerate to form two-dimensional vacancy loops, which collapse into dislocation loops, or three-dimensional clusters called voids. This difference in behavior between interstitials and vacancies has an important effect on determining the swelling that many metals suffer as a result of exposure to fast neutrons and other particle radiation over a certain temperature range. When irradiation-induced swelling occurs, it is usually significant only in the temperature range of roughly 0.3 T_m to 0.5 T_m, where T_m is the melting point of the metal in Kelvin degrees.

Swelling can also result from gases produced in materials, such as helium formed by (n,α) reactions and other gaseous impurities present in the metals. These traces of gas increase the concentration of voids formed upon exposure to radiation. For example, the (n,α) and (n,2n) reactions between fast neutrons and beryllium form helium and tritium gases that create swelling.

Under certain conditions, embrittlement can be enhanced by the presence of the helium bubbles (helium embrittlement). The accepted view is that this embrittlement is the result of stress-induced growth of helium gas bubbles at the grain boundaries. The bubbles eventually link up and cause intergranular failure.

Fissionable metals suffer from radiation damage in a manner similar to that encountered in structural alloys. Additional problems are introduced by the high energy fission fragments and the heavy gases xenon and krypton, which appear among the fission products. Two fragments that share 167 MeV of kinetic energy, in inverse proportion to their atomic masses, are produced from each fission. Each fragment will have a range of several hundred angstroms as it produces a displacement spike. A core of vacancies is surrounded by a shell of interstitials, producing growth and distortion. Figure 6 shows the growth in a uranium rod upon irradiation.

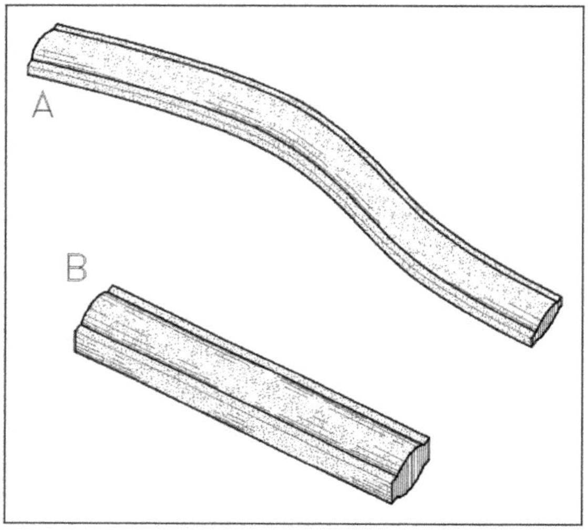

The gas formation produces eventual swelling of the fuel and may place the cladding under considerable pressure as well. One of the major challenges in alloying metallic uranium is the attainment of better stability under irradiation. Small additions of zirconium have shown marked improvement in reducing growth and distortion.

Figure 6 (a) Growth of Uranium Rod; (b) Uranium Rod Size Dummy

The physical effects of ionizing radiation in metals is a uniform heating of the metal. Ions are produced by the passage of gamma rays or charged particles through the metal, causing sufficient electrical interaction to remove an external (or orbital) electron from the atom. Metals with shared electrons, which are relatively free to wander through the crystal lattice, are effected very little by ionization.

EFFECT DUE TO NEUTRON CAPTURE

Summary

The important information in this chapter is summarized below.

Effect Due To Neutron Capture Summary

- Dislocation of an atom due to emission of radiation

    Highly energetic recoil nuclei are produced indirectly by the absorption of a neutron and subsequent emission of a γ-ray. When the γ-ray is emitted, the atom recoils due to the reaction of the nucleus to the γ-ray's momentum (conservation of momentum).

- Effects from capture

    Introduction of impurity atom due to the transmutation of the absorbing nucleus.

    Atomic displacement due to recoil atoms or knock-ons

- Thermal neutrons cannot produce displacements directly, but can indirectly as a result of radiative capture and other neutron reactions or elastic scattering.

RADIATION EFFECTS IN ORGANIC COMPOUNDS

As described previously, the effects of gamma and beta radiation on metal are not permanent. On the other hand, organic material will suffer permanent damage as its chemical bonds are broken by incident gamma and beta radiation. This chapter discusses how radiation effects organic compounds.

EO 1.23   **STATE how gamma and beta radiation effect organic materials.**

EO 1.24   **IDENTIFY the change in organic compounds due to radiation.**

       a.   Nylon
       b.   High-density polyethylene marlex 50
       c.   Rubber

EO 1.25   **IDENTIFY the chemical bond with the least resistance to radiation.**

EO 1.26   **DEFINE the term polymerization.**

Radiation Effects

Incident gamma and beta radiation causes very little damage in metals, but will break the chemical bonds and prevent bond recombination of organic compounds and cause permanent damage. Ionization is the major damage mechanism in organic compounds. Ionization effects are caused by the passage through a material of gamma rays or charged particles such as beta and alpha particles. Even fast neutrons, producing fast protons on collision, lead to ionization as a major damage mechanism. For thermal neutrons the major effect is through (n,gamma) reactions with hydrogen, with the 2.2 MeV gamma producing energetic electrons and ionization. Ionization is particularly important with materials that have either ionic or covalent bonding.

Ion production within a chemical compound is accomplished by the breaking of chemical bonds. This radiation-induced decomposition prevents the use of many compounds in a reactor environment. Materials such as insulators, dielectrics, plastics, lubricants, hydraulic fluids, and rubber are among those that are sensitive to ionization. Plastics with long-chain-type molecules having varying amounts of cross-linking may have sharp changes in properties due to irradiation. In general, plastics suffer varying degrees of loss in their properties after exposure to high radiation fields. Nylon begins to suffer degradation of its toughness at relatively low doses, but suffers little loss in strength.

High-density (linear) polyethylene marlex 50 loses both strength and ductility at relatively low doses. In general, rubber will harden upon being irradiated. However, butyl or Thiokol rubber will soften or become liquid with high radiation doses.

It is important that oils and greases be evaluated for their resistance to radiation if they are to be employed in a high-radiation environment. Liquids that have the aromatic ring-type structure show an inherent radiation resistance and are well suited to be used as lubricants or hydraulics.

For a given gamma flux, the degree of decomposition observed depends on the type of chemical bonding present. The chemical bond with the least resistance to decomposition is the *covalent bond*. In a covalent bond, the outer, or valence, electrons are shared by two atoms rather than being firmly attached to any one atom. Organic compounds, and some inorganic compounds such as water, exhibit this type of bonding. There is considerable variation in the strength of covalent bonds present in compounds of different types and therefore a wide variation in their stability under radiation. The plastics discussed above can show very sharp property changes with radiation, whereas polyphenyls are reasonably stable.

One result of ionization is that smaller hydrocarbon chains will be formed (lighter hydrocarbons and gases) as well as heavier hydrocarbons by recombination of broken chains into larger ones. This recombination of broken hydrocarbon chains into longer ones is called *polymerization*.

Polymerization is one of the chemical reactions that takes place in organic compounds during irradiation and is responsible for changes in the properties of this material. Some other chemical reactions in organic compounds that can be caused by radiation are oxidation, halogenation, and changes in isomerism. The polymerization mechanism is used in some industrial applications to change the character of plastics after they are in place; for example, wood is impregnated with a light plastic and then cross-bonded (polymerized) by irradiating it to make it more sturdy. This change in properties, whether it be a lubricant, electrical insulation, or gaskets, is of concern when choosing materials for use near nuclear reactors. One of the results of the Three Mile Island accident is that utilities have been asked to evaluate whether instrumentation would function in the event of radiation exposure being spread because of an accident.

Because neutrons and gamma rays (and other nuclear radiations) produce the same kind of decomposition in organic compounds, it is common to express the effects as a function of the energy absorbed. One way is to state the energy in terms of a unit called the rad. The *rad* represents an energy absorption of 100 ergs per gram of material. As an example of the effects of radiation, Figure 7 shows the increase in viscosity with radiation exposure (in rads) of three organic compounds that might be considered for use as reactor moderators and coolants.

The ordinates represent the viscosity increase relative to that of the material before irradiation (mostly at 100°F), so that they give a general indication of the extent of decomposition due to radiation exposure. This figure illustrates that aromatic hydrocarbons (n-butyl benzene) are more resistant to radiation damage than are aliphatic compounds (hexadecane). The most resistant of all are the polyphenyls, of which diphenyl is the simplest example.

Plant Materials   RADIATION EFFECTS IN ORGANIC COMPOUNDS

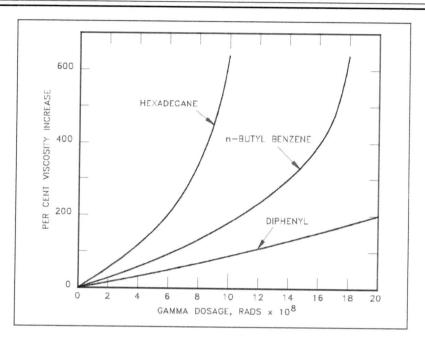

Figure 7 Effect of Gamma Radiation on
Different Types of Hydrocarbon

The stability of organic (and other covalent) compounds to radiation is frequently expressed by means of the "G" value, which is equal to the number of molecules decomposed, or of product formed, per 100 eV of energy dissipated in the material. As an example of the use of G values, the data in Table 3 are for a number of polyphenyls exposed to the radiation in a thermal reactor.

The table shows the number of gas molecules produced, G(gas), and the number of polyphenyl molecules, G(polymer), used to produce higher polymers per 100 eV of energy deposited in the material. Note that this adds up to approximately 1000 atoms of gas and 10,000 atoms forming higher polymers per each 1 MeV particle. It is also of interest to note that the terphenyls are even more resistant to radiation than diphenyl and, since they have a higher boiling point, a mixture of terphenyls with a relatively low melting temperature was chosen as the moderator-coolant in organic-moderated reactors.

TABLE 3
Radiolytic Decomposition of Polyphenyls at 350°C

Material	G (gas)	G (polymer)
Diphenyl	0.159	1.13
Ortho-terphenyl	0.108	0.70
Meta-terphenyl	0.081	0.64
Para-terphenyl	0.073	0.54
Santowax-R*	0.080	0.59

* A mixture of the three terphenyls plus a small amount of diphenyl.

An effect similar to that described above occurs in water molecules that are decomposed by radiation into hydrogen and oxygen in a reactor. Control of oxygen produced by this process is an important part of reactor chemistry.

Summary

The important information in this chapter is summarized below.

Radiation Effects in Organic Compounds Summary

- Gamma and beta radiation have little effect on metals, but break the chemical bonds and prevent bond recombination of organic compounds and cause permanent damage.

- Radiation causes changes in organic materials.

    Nylon has a degradation of its toughness at relatively low doses and little loss of strength.

    High-density (linear) polyethylene marlex 50 loses both strength and ductility at relatively low doses.

    Typically rubber increases in hardness when irradiated. Butyl or Thiokol rubber soften or become liquid with high radiation doses.

- The chemical bond with the least amount of resistance to radiation is the covalent bond.

- Polymerization is the recombining of broken hydrocarbon chains into longer ones.

REACTOR USE OF ALUMINUM

Aluminum is a favorite material for applications in tritium production and reactor plants. This chapter discusses the applications of aluminum in a reactor plant.

EO 1.27 STATE the applications and the property that makes aluminum ideally suited for use in reactors operating at:

    a. Low kilowatt power
    b. Low temperature ranges.
    c. Moderate temperature range

EO 1.28 STATE why aluminum is undesirable in high temperature power reactors.

Applications

Aluminum, with its low cost, low thermal neutron absorption, and freedom from corrosion at low temperature, is ideally suited for use in research or training reactors in the low kilowatt power and low temperature operating ranges.

Aluminum, usually in the relatively pure (greater than 99.0%) 2S (or 1100) form, has been extensively used as a reactor structural material and for fuel cladding and other purposes not involving exposure to very high temperatures.

Aluminum with its low neutron capture cross section (0.24 barns) is the preferred cladding material for pressurized and boiling water reactors operating in the moderate temperature range. Aluminum, in the form of an APM alloy, is generally used as a fuel-element cladding in organic-moderated reactors. Aluminum has also been employed in gas-cooled reactors operating at low or moderately high temperatures. Generally, at high temperatures, the relative low strength and poor corrosion properties of aluminum make it unsuitable as a structural material in power reactors due to hydrogen generation. The high temperature strength and corrosion properties of aluminum can be increased by alloying, but only at the expense of a higher neutron capture cross section.

In water, corrosion limits the use of aluminum to temperatures near 100°C, unless special precautions are taken. In air, corrosion limits its use to temperatures slightly over 300°C. Failure is caused by pitting of the otherwise protective $Al(OH)_3$ film. The presence of chloride salts and of some other metals that form strong galvanic couples (for example, copper) can promote pitting.

Aluminum is attacked by both water and steam at temperatures above about 150°C, but this temperature can be raised by alloying with small percentages of up to 1.0% Fe (iron) and 2.5% Ni (nickel). These alloys are known as aerial alloys. The mechanism of attack is attributed to the reaction $Al + 3H_2O \rightarrow Al(OH)_3 + 3H^+$ when the hydrogen ions diffuse through the hydroxide layer and, on recombination, disrupt the adhesion of the protective coating.

Aluminum-uranium alloys have been used as fuel elements in several research reactors. Enriched uranium is alloyed with 99.7% pure aluminum to form the alloy.

Research has shown that radiation produces changes in both annealed and hardened aluminum and its alloys. Yield strength and tensile strength increase with irradiation. Data indicates that yield strengths of annealed alloys are more effected by irradiation than tensile strengths. The yield strengths and the tensile strengths of hardened alloys undergo about the same percent increase as a result of irradiation. Irradiation tends to decrease the ductility of alloys. Stress-strain curves for an irradiated and an unirradiated control specimen are shown in Figure 8. Figure 8 illustrates the effect of neutron irradiation in increasing the yield strength and the tensile strength and in decreasing ductility.

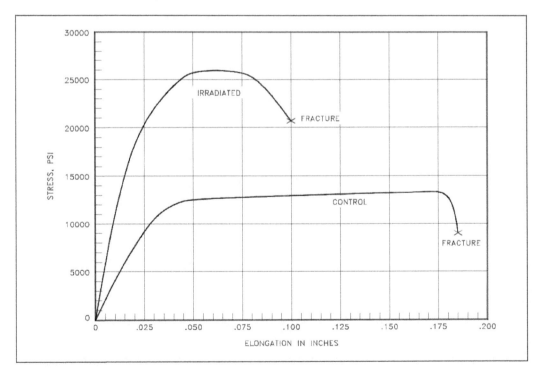

Figure 8 Effect of Irradiation on Tensile Properties of 2SO Aluminum

Plant Materials   REACTOR USE OF ALUMINUM

Summary

The important information in this chapter is summarized below.

Reactor Use of Aluminum Summary

- Aluminum is ideally suited for use in low kilowatt power and low temperature reactors due to its low cost, low thermal neutron absorption, and freedom from corrosion at low temperatures.

- Aluminum, with its low neutron capture cross section is the preferred cladding material for moderate temperature ranges.

- Aluminum has been ruled out for power reactor application due to hydrogen generation and it does not have adequate mechanical and corrosion-resistant properties at the high operating temperatures.

Milton Keynes UK
Ingram Content Group UK Ltd.
UKHW031345220724
42UKWH00063B/876